WIZARD® BIG COVERS BOOK

It's a book about covers.
And it's big.

CHAIRMAN *Gareb S. Shamus* ■ **PRESIDENT/COO** *Fred Pierce* ■ **VICE PRESIDENT/EDITOR-IN-CHIEF** *Patrick McCallum*
VP/CFO *Edward L. DuPré* ■ **VP/BUSINESS DEVELOPMENT** *Martha Donato* ■ **VP/ADVERTISING DIRECTOR** *Ken Scrudato*
CREATIVE DIRECTOR *Steve Blackwell* ■ **EDITOR** *Brian Cunningham* ■ **SENIOR MANAGING EDITOR** *Joe Yanarella*
PRODUCTION DIRECTOR *Darren Sanchez* ■ **DIRECTOR OF CIRCULATION** *Tom Conboy* ■ **DIRECTOR OF SALES** *Stewart Morales*
RESEARCH EDITOR *Daniel Reilly* ■ **COPY EDITORS** *Joshua Elder & Trisha L. Sebastian*

INTRODUCTION

By Joe Quesada

THE COVER SELLS.

Don't kid yourself. It's the superstars like Brian Michael Bendis and John Romita Jr. that keep you coming back, but whether you're talking about comic books or magazines, the cover sells. When somebody walks into a store, the first thing they see is the cover. When somebody walks past a newsstand, it's the cover that catches their eye.

The cover is what entices someone to pick a book up off the shelf, and as such, it's an unbelievably important part—arguably, the *most* important part—of selling a product. We are constantly judging our books by their covers.

When I went into a comic shop after years and years of not reading comics, there was only one book that caught my eye—and only one book I bought—*Watchmen*. I didn't know what or who Moore and Gibbons were, but that cover—WOW! It was so unique for its time. It had that big "Watchmen" running in a band down the left side—it was just so darn unusual compared to everything else on the stands. What made it so captivating…its key to success (at least its success with me) was its simplicity.

Simplicity sells.

There was a time in this industry when cover blurbs—big, bold graphics stating what was in that issue—were important. It was a monthly business on the newsstand, and you wanted people to know the difference between one comic and the next. But most stuff on the newsstand was pretty much the same. Comics were only keeping in step with the modern publishing world.

Times changed, but for the longest time comics refused to. We became so insular that we would willingly follow tradition to the grave. We forgot the lessons taught to us by our predecessors. It's not about reverence, it's about relevance.

Look at the world of modern-day publishing. Look at what all the major magazine publishers feature on their covers—it's usually one very simple, iconic image. A pretty model, a famous athlete, even celebrities can do the trick. You very rarely see a team of people on a cover, unless it has something to do with an ensemble show like "Friends" (and even then, they keep the composition simple.) For the most part, it's a single figure or a single, simple, iconic graphic.

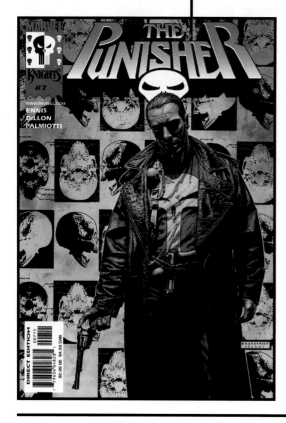

Sure, from time to time it's okay to throw in a story cover, but it's not the best way to catch a customer's eye. For example, Marvel used to try to fit every one of the X-Men onto every *X-Men* cover. But once you got every X-Man on the cover—each wearing their different color uniform, doing a different action, using a different power and each power with a different color—you ended up with something that looked like a pizza pie with everything on it. There was no way, no matter how well you designed it, that a cover like that was going to hold together, no way it would stand out on the stands. People may look at what appears to be a simple cover and think it was a no-brainer and easy to design, but they couldn't be more wrong. It's actually easier to design an image with many elements or characters, but when it comes to covers, quantity doesn't necessarily equate to quality.

Tim Bradstreet's great at creating simple, yet effective covers. From a purely graphic perspective, all of his *Punisher* covers **[one shown at left]** are kind of the same if you look at the elements. It's the Punisher, standing around holding a gun in one form or fashion, yet Tim takes it to another level. In that respect, he's probably one of the best designers in the history of comics—he's able to take one simple Punisher graphic and, every month, do something with only a few elements to make each cover completely and totally unique.

Alex Ross gets it. He's always good for a dramatic punch because of his ultra-, hyper-realistic style and his sense of drama. If he puts more than one character on a cover, he generally puts them in a nice, stacked, one-behind-the-other orderly pose. He'll usually use a kid's-eye perspective to make his characters larger than life, to give us that same sense of wonder we all had when we cracked open our first superhero comic.

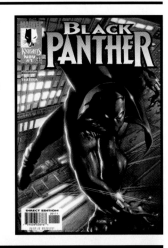

Look back at the Marvel Knights launch—the first issues for the original four series were all highly calculated. We knew they would be the pieces everyone would be seeing, ad nauseum, until the books were released. With the exception of *Inhumans* (and there's an argument for that one, see Alex Ross), all the images were simple, iconic, single characters standing in full pose. Those covers were memorable. They were seen everywhere, they were used everywhere, because they were so simple. To this day, that *Black Panther* #1 cover by Mark Texiera **[top right]** is the greatest piece of Black Panther art—EVER!

Then there's *Wizard*.

Wizard's covers have come a long way since the magazine began. Back in the early days, *Wizard* was doing things like gatefolds and going for big, splashy action covers. I remember getting cover assignments where they'd say things like, "We want Spider-Man battling the Lizard and the Hobgoblin and...so on."

Somewhere down the road, *Wizard* changed its art direction. The mandate matured from "Make 'em big and splashy" to "Keep them iconic and simple." Even if you were using multiple characters, *Wizard* wanted them very simplistically arranged. They wanted to make sure the layout wasn't getting too convoluted and in the way of itself. Ironically, by virtue of making them simple, *Wizard*'s covers actually ended up being bigger and splashier.

I'll never forget when they changed gears. I said "What do you mean I have to shove everything to the right?" (*Wizard* now asks its cover artists to keep their artwork as flush to the right as possible, so they can run their text down the left-hand side of the cover.) Still, being a good boy, I followed instructions. (Hey, just cause I'm EIC doesn't mean I get a free ride.)

When I was done, I couldn't help but feel dissatisfied with the overall piece I had drawn. It felt awkwardly unbalanced, since everything was crammed off to one side. "Hey," I told myself, "it's their magazine."

When I saw the final product, though, I was thrilled. I immediately understood that their mandate was no different from the one I was establishing at Marvel.

The cover sells.

Quesada -2003-

Joe Quesada

An award-winning cover artist in his own right, Joe Quesada remains an industry leader as Marvel Comics' editor-in-chief.

BY THE NUMBERS

Eight years, one magazine, 165 covers. Let's see what other cool stuff we can come up with when we get a bunch of interns to sit in a windowless room and flip through *Wizard* back issues*.

Character who's appeared on the most covers (Wolverine)	20
Batman covers	19
Superman covers	17
Spider-Man covers	17
Superman/Spider-Man team-up covers	3
Hulk covers	11
X-Men covers	10
JLA covers	6
Covers of a fat guy eating mac 'n' cheese	0
Artist who's drawn the most covers (Bart Sears)	11
Alex Ross covers	10
Jim Lee covers	9
Joe Quesada covers	8
Covers that have a "Hey, let's wear a wizard hat!" theme	20
Covers before we realized that theme was stupid	20
Cover that got us in the most trouble	10
Single panel covers	129
Gatefold covers	30
Triple-gatefold covers	6
Double-secret quintuple-gatefold covers	**
Most characters on a single cover (Issue #83)	33
Pieces of artwork that appear in this volume	306
Staffers who appeared on covers (Gareb, on issue #34. Hey...he pays the bills)	1

A special thanks to Steve Blackwell, Arlene So, Brad Fountain, Matt Tierney, Leo McCarthy and all the artists and designers who made this book possible. We'd say you were the best, but then we'd have to pay you more.

* Final tallies correspond to Wizard #1-#100 (including issue #2000).
** We can't say. It's a double-secret.   PRINTED IN CANADA

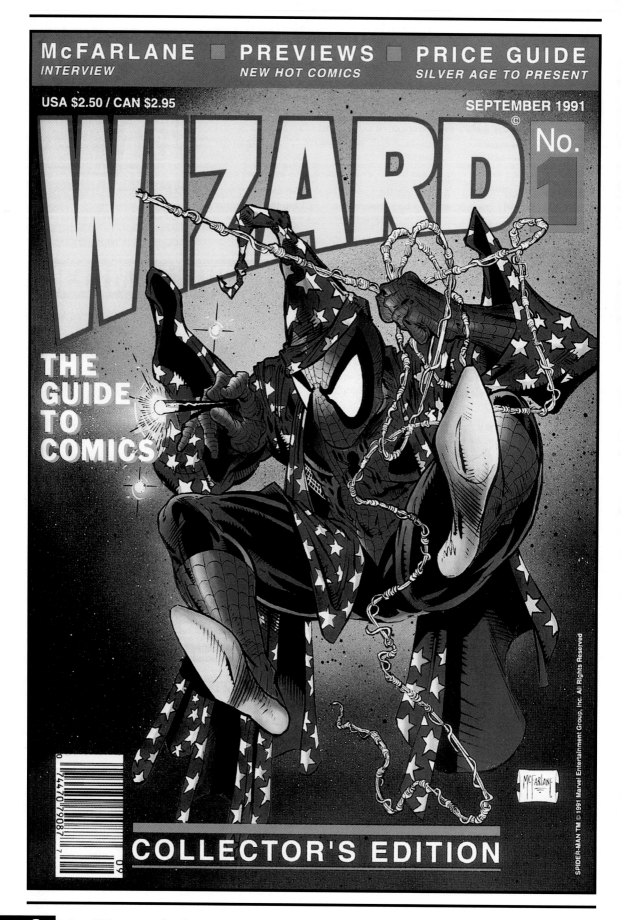

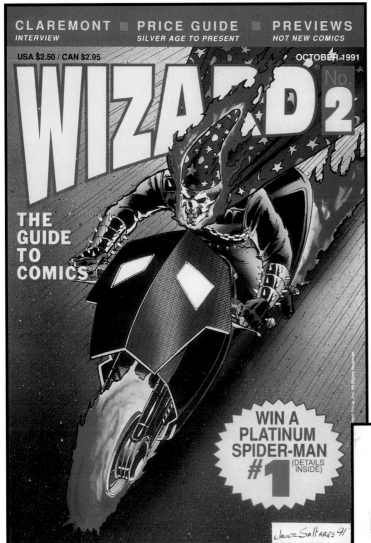

Javier Saltares 91

GHOST RIDER ™

1 SPIDER-MAN (September 1991)
PENCILER/INKER: Todd McFarlane
COLORIST: Mark H. McNabb

A year before the launch of the magazine, *Wizard* founder Gareb Shanus gave his dad—an original art buff—a pretty kickass gift: an original Todd McFarlane Spider-Man. Why the pointy hat and robe? An homage to the comic store his father once owned called "The Wizard of Cards & Comics," a name that would go on to inspire the title of the magazine. With McFarlane's blessing, it would become the cover to issue #1.

2 GHOST RIDER (October 1991)
PENCILER/INKER: Javier Saltares
COLORIST: Mark H. McNabb

We originally asked Jim Lee to draw us a Wolverine cover, but Lee couldn't commit due to the demanding schedule of his impending *X-Men* launch. We kept the door open until our deadline in hopes of snagging him anyway, but it just didn't work out. Scrambling like headless chickens for a new cover, we turned to Javier Saltares—a rising star and hot up-and-comer on *Ghost Rider*. He was so excited about the project, he did two covers **[above right]**. We cut our deadline so close that we had to drive 40 miles to his Bronx flat to pick up the cover art personally.

BISLEY
INTERVIEW

PRICE GUIDE
SILVER AGE TO PRESENT

NEW TOP 100
THE HOTTEST COMICS

USA $2.50 / CAN $2.95

NOVEMBER 1991

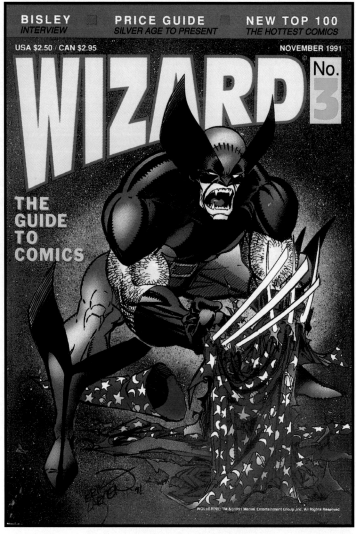

WIZARD

No. 3

THE
GUIDE
TO
COMICS

3 WOLVERINE (November 1991)
PENCILER/INKER: Erik Larsen
COLORIST: Mark H. McNabb

Still looking for that elusive Wolverine cover, we approached artist Rob Liefeld. After his deadline came and went, we continued our proud headless-chicken tradition and—at the eleventh hour—found our saving grace in the art of Erik Larsen, who was already hard at work wrapping up a Lobo cover for us **[top left]**. While Lobo would ultimately never run, Larsen turned around this, the first ever Wolverine cover on *Wizard*, in a few hours.

4 BATMAN (December 1991)
PENCILER/INKER: Bart Sears
COLORIST: Mark H. McNabb

The first DC Comics (and non-Marvel) *Wizard* cover. We asked Bart to draw some of DC's big guns, and his first two were Batman and Wonder Woman **[at right]**, the latter of which never ran. Our motif at the time had been to feature characters wearing a wizard hat and robe, though DC informed us that it would not look favorably upon its characters depicted that way. That's why Batman—and all DC characters since—never touched *Wizard* colors.

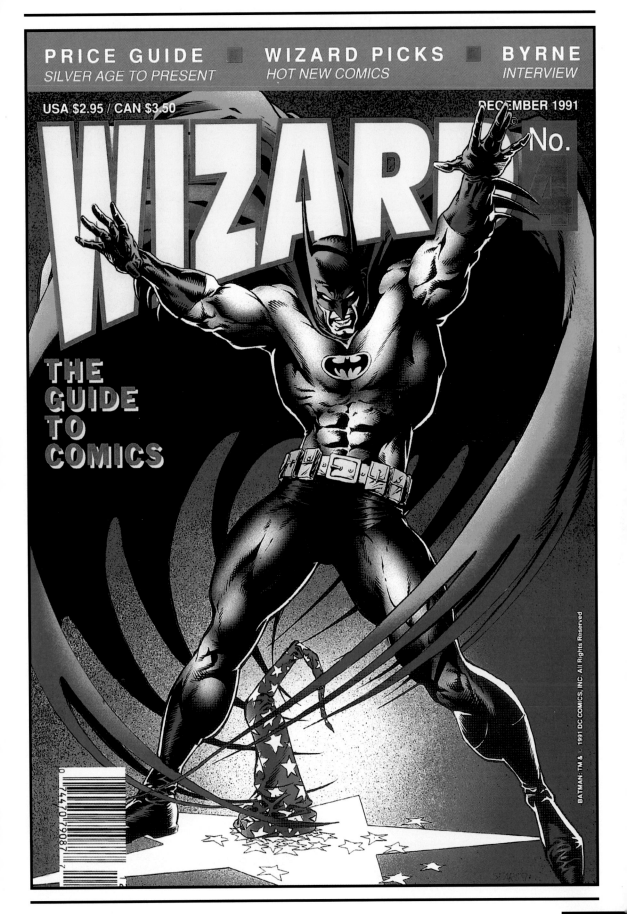

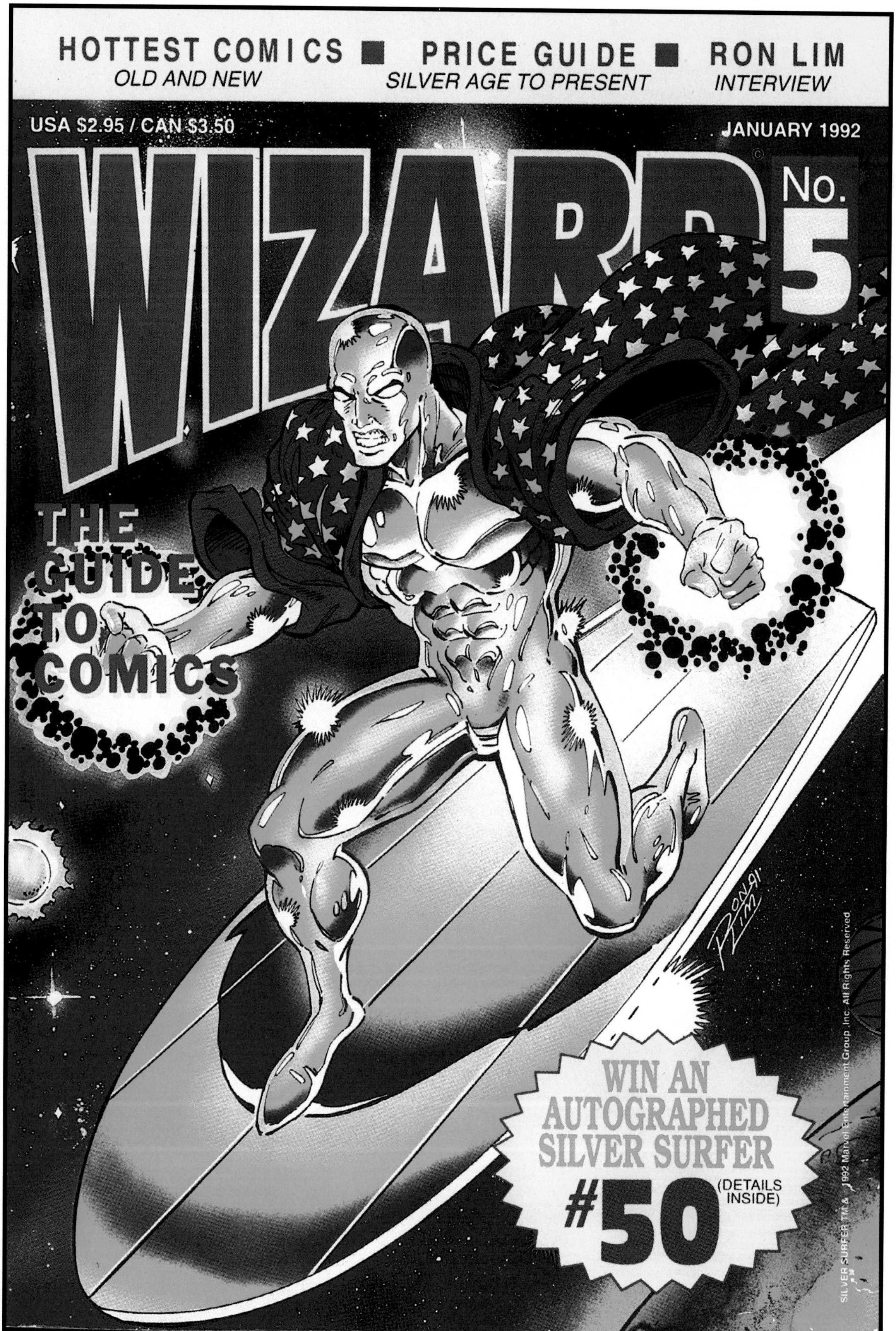
HOTTEST COMICS
OLD AND NEW
PRICE GUIDE
SILVER AGE TO PRESENT
RON LIM
INTERVIEW
USA $2.95 / CAN $3.50
JANUARY 1992
WIZARD
No. 5
THE GUIDE TO COMICS
WIN AN AUTOGRAPHED SILVER SURFER #50
(DETAILS INSIDE)
SILVER SURFER TM & © 1992 Marvel Entertainment Group, Inc. All Rights Reserved

5 SILVER SURFER (January 1992)
PENCILER/INKER: Ron Lim
COLORIST: Mark H. McNabb

Orignally slated to be a Silver Surfer vs. Thanos cover, that idea was scrapped in favor of a larger, single character image. Having a big, billowing cloak made the Surfer look all the more naked.

Oftentimes we assigned two covers at once. Unfortunately for painter Joe Jusko, his Deathlok cover **[at left]** didn't make the cut because of the character's waning popularity.

6 THE HULK (February 1992)
PENCILER/INKER: Sam Kieth
COLORIST: Mark H. McNabb

Although *Wizard* has been printed with two distinct covers on every issue since 1995, the idea was tested for the first time in '92. We distributed a limited variant cover (10 percent of the print run), which featured a gray Hulk instead of green. No one noticed. (This would also be the first time characters on our cover interacted with design elements like the *Wizard* logo.)

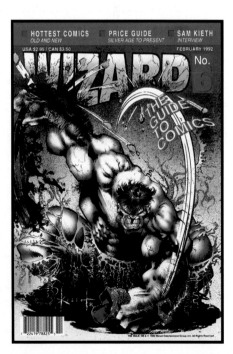

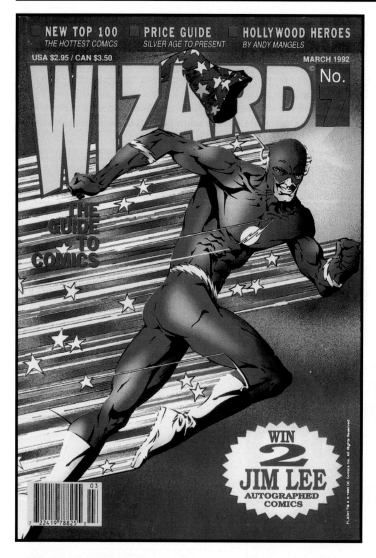

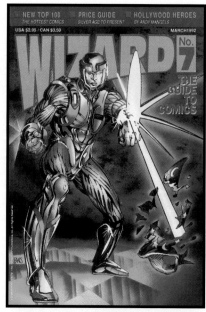

7 THE FLASH (March 1992)
PENCILER/INKER: Bart Sears
COLORIST: Mark H. McNabb

Concerned that fans may not recognize Valiant Comics' new X-O character (who?), we went with our first distinct "split cover"—as it's known in
the biz—with Flash. Split covers would become the norm with issue #45.

7A X-O MANOWAR (March 1992)
PENCILER/INKER: Barry Windsor-Smith
COLORIST: Mark H. McNabb

8 BISHOP (April 1992)
PENCILER/INKER: Whilce Portacio
COLORIST: Mark H. McNabb

Bishop: tougher than kryptonite. Midway through the production cycle of
#8, Marvel asked if we were interested in debuting its new X-Man on our
cover. This not only represented the first time a major publisher reached
out to us, but it was our very first exclusive story, to boot. Too good to
pass up, we KO'd our Superman cover (a split cover, as we learned with
#7, proved too expensive at the time) by Bart Sears **[bottom right]**, and
the Man of Steel would somehow elude a *Wizard* cover until issue #47.

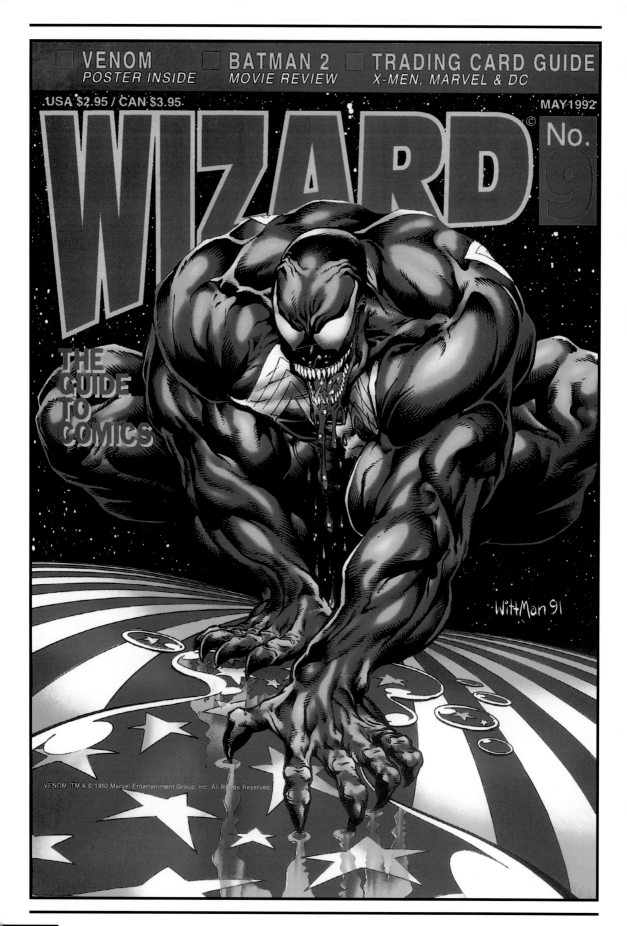

9 VENOM (May 1992)
PENCILER/INKER: Bart Sears (drawing as Wittman)
COLORIST: Mark H. McNabb

Our first villain cover. Determining that the Joker art **[at left]** didn't show enough of the Clown Prince of Crime, we switched gears and went with a different villain: Marvel Comics' Venom. Bart Sears—who drew both images—was locked into a DC-exclusive contract at the time and used his middle name ("Wittman") as a pen name.

10 CABLE AND SHAFT (June 1992)
PENCILER/INKER: Rob Liefeld
COLORIST: Mark H. McNabb

To date, the most challenging *Wizard* cover of all time. Originally planned as a Sandman cover by Kelley Jones **[bottom right]**, Rob Liefeld called at the eleventh hour to confess he wasn't having fun drawing the Sabretooth cover we assigned him a few months prior. He requested to draw another mutant: Cable. Having chased Liefeld for a cover since issue #3—and with his assurances that he'd complete the cover on time— we rescheduled Sandman (though it would never see print). As the deadline loomed, his cover arrived with two surprises: it was drawn to incorrect cover specs, and alongside Cable stood Liefeld's new Image Comics character Shaft. When Marvel execs—still burning from Liefeld's acrimonious exit to form Image—caught wind of this, they urged us to rethink the cover. While the matter was settled amicably with the cover shipping unchanged, Liefeld's artwork—which had to be altered to fit our cover specs— remained a sore topic with Marvel for a little while and has only been shown in print once before.

YOUNGBLOOD #0
TRADING CARD ENCLOSED

ROB LIEFELD
INTERVIEW

SPIDEY
POSTER

USA $2.95 / CAN $3.95   JUNE 1992

WIZARD

THE GUIDE TO COMICS

11 SPAWN (July 1992)
PENCILER/INKER: Todd McFarlane
COLORIST: Mark H. McNabb

With a fan frenzy surrounding the newly created Image Comics, Todd McFarlane offered us an early look at Spawn, which bumped the planned cover featuring Marvel UK's surprise hit Death's Head II by Liam Sharpe and Cam Smith **[above left]**. McFarlane gave us an early design sketch for Spawn that was inked and colored for use as this cover. Note the beaded armbands, a concept that would be changed to spikes for the character's final design.

12 WILDC.A.T.S (August 1992)
PENCILER: Jim Lee
INKER: Scott Williams
COLORIST: Mark H. McNabb

Jim Lee called and said that he not only had time to draw that Wolverine cover **[at right]** we'd been after him for since issue #2, but that he was going to draw us *two covers.* The condition: we had to run his creator-owned WildC.A.T.s cover first (with Emp, Warblade and Zealot). Not being stupid, we said yes. The prized Wolverine vs. Sabretooth cover was held for years to be used in an amorphous "special event" issue…that never materialized.

GHOST RIDER ■ COMICS WORLD ■ PRICE GUIDE
POSTER   COMES TO TV   SILVER AGE TO PRESENT
USA $3.95 / CAN $4.95   SEPTEMBER 1992
WIZARD™
No. 13
THE GUIDE TO COMICS
FLASH! FLASH! FLASH! FLASH! FLASH!
WIZARD WINNER 1991
BEST NEW PUBLISHER
OF THE YEAR !!!
GHOST RIDER: ®&TM 1992 Marvel Entertainment Group. All Rights Reserved.

13 **GHOST RIDER** (September 1992)
PAINTER: Nelson
First painted cover. We had Nelson paint two potential covers—a Juggernaut/Hulk **[top right]** and Ghost Rider. We went with the latter, easily the more dynamic of the two. And contrary to what most staffers thought at the time, that's a burning wizard cap, not a flaming traffic cone. Moments like this makes us wonder why we ever thought that the wizard hat and robe motif was a good idea.

14 **X-WOMEN** (October 1992)
PENCILER/INKER: Art Thibert
COLORIST: Mark H. McNabb
On this cover we wanted sex appeal. She-Hulk's solo title at the time had a strong cult following and we turned to definitive Shulkie artist John Byrne for a cover **[bottom right]**. It was later decided for sales reasons to go with the more popular X-Men (or in this case, X-Women) but to keep the cheesecake motif. Originally slated to be a sultry shot of Storm, Rogue, Psylocke and Jean Grey, a breakdown in communications with the artist led to those characters being relegated to the background and Jubilee taking center stage.

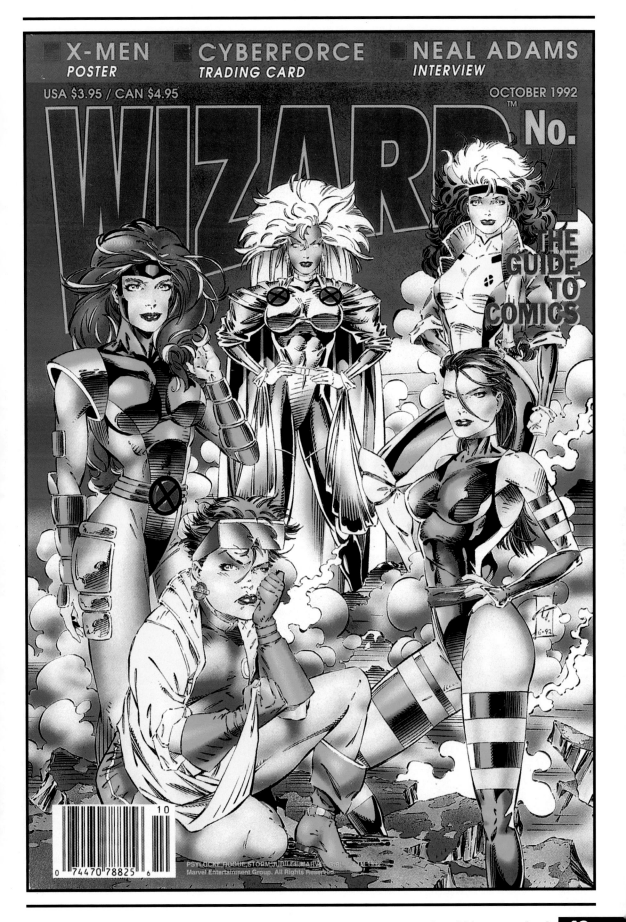

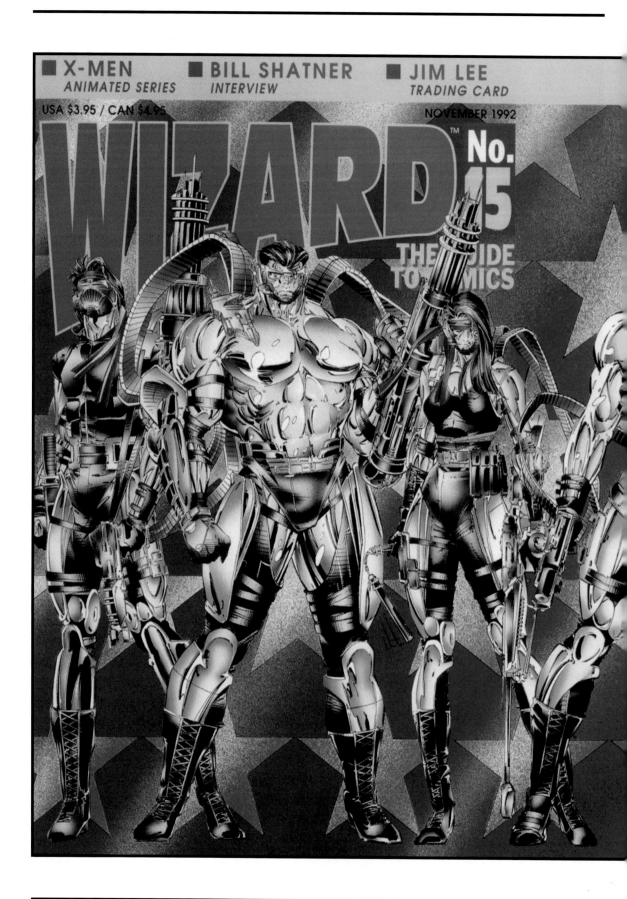

WIZARD COVERS IT ALL!

15 WETWORKS
(November 1992)
PENCILER/INKER: Whilce Portacio
COLORIST: Mark H. McNabb

After Whilce Portacio had drafted a dozen sketches that were rejected for the cover (all of which were thrown away by accident), *Wizard* head honcho Gareb Shamus spotted a stack of WetWorks full-body character designs of (from left) Grail, Claymore, Pilgrim, Jester and Dozer. Liking what he saw, he asked Portacio to link the drawings into one piece of art and ink it as a single image. The result was the first *Wizard* fold-out cover—known in the biz as a "gatefold cover"—a trend that would run off and on (mostly on) until the last gatefold cover to date, issue #83.

The Maxx: © & TM 1992 Sam Kieth
The Pitt: © & TM 1992 Dale Keown
Deathblow: © & TM 1992 Jim Lee
Bloodwulf: © & TM 1992 Rob Liefeld
All Rights Reserved

THE MAXX

16 DARKER IMAGE (December 1992)

PENCILERS/INKERS: Sam Kieth, Dale Keown, Jim Lee, Rob Liefeld
COLORIST: Mark H. McNabb

Refusing to let a good idea die (read: the *Wizard* staff was 95 percent male at the time), we went back to the gamma well for another sexy She-Hulk cover. This time we turned to Bart Sears for two She-Hulk cover variants—one for Eastern U.S. comic stores **[top right]**, the other for Western U.S. stores **[bottom right]**—and the directions we gave were to draw "over-the-top sexy." And he delivered…in spades. While provocative, we felt the images were a bit much for our all-ages mag.

Image countered with a jam art piece featuring characters from its upcoming *Darker Image* anthology title (from left: The Maxx, Pitt, Deathblow and Bloodwulf) drawn by four different art teams. Jam covers (i.e., one cover featuring multiple artists) have the tendency to look a bit muddled, but we acquiesced when told *Darker Image* would be heavily promoted. To date, only one issue of that series has shipped.

"Darker Image"

R COVERAGE IS ABSOLUTE"

17 VALIANT UNIVERSE
(January 1993)
PENCILER: David Lapham

INKER: Bob Layton
COLORIST: Mark H. McNabb

This would be the first issue of *Wizard* produced in the "official" offices after the company moved out of bossman Gareb Shamus' living room.

Hot on the heels of its staggering $2 million grossing *Bloodshot* #1, Valiant stood at the peak of its popularity. We asked Valiant's rising star David Lapham to draw us this cover with (from left) Bloodshot, Solar, X-O, Magnus, Zephyr, Armstrong and Archer.

Late in the production of this ish, Now Comics sent us a Green Hornet cover by Tod Smith and Rick Magyar **[above]** completely unsolicited in the hope of promoting its new series. Neat cover, but we couldn't accommodate a gatefold/non-gatefold variant due to advertising commitments (the interior front cover had been sold as a gatefold ad). The *Hornet* series ended shortly thereafter, and to date this marks the closest the Green Hornet—or that lil' Kato fella—have ever been to being featured on a *Wizard* cover.

ACHNID IN A HARD PLACE"

18 SPIDER-MAN
(February 1993)
PENCILER/INKER: Bart Sears (as Wittman)
COLORIST: Mark H. McNabb

No, we don't know why we had a Darkhawk cover by Bart Sears commissioned either **[below]**. Let this be a lesson to you kids: stay off the dope!

Revisiting Venom from his wildly popular *Wizard* #9 cover, Sears upped the ante by mixing in Spider-Man and the then-red-hot villain Carnage.

Bart had since signed a more liberal contract with Valiant, and could now draw whatever he wanted—but he kept the Wittman pseudonym anyway.

The *Wizard* design department also tested the placement of the magazine's "The Guide to Comics" tagline, an experiment that lasted all of one issue.

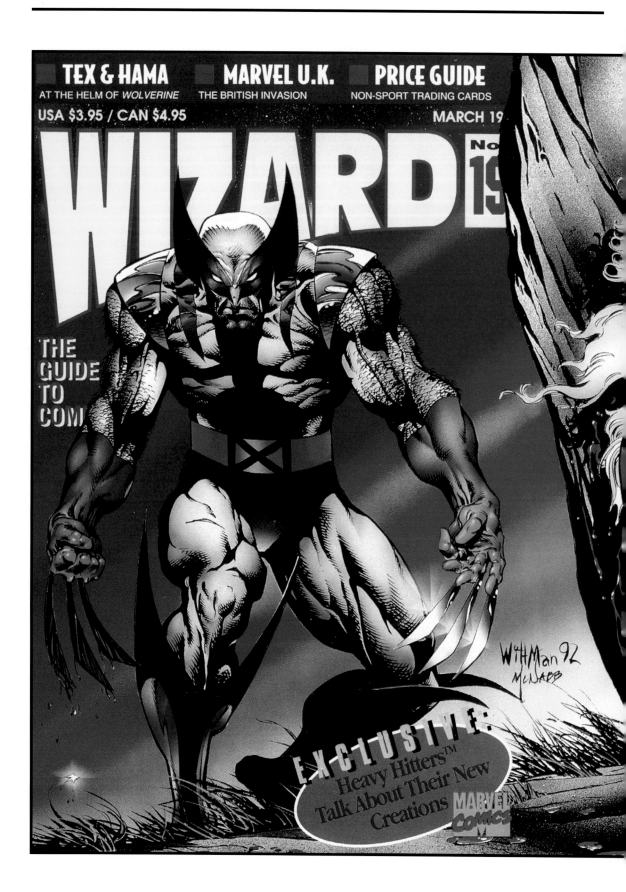

Wolverine & Sabretooth: © &TM Marvel Entertainment Group. All Rights Reserved

19

WOLVERINE (March 1993)
PENCILER/INKER: Bart Sears (as Wittman)
COLORIST: Mark H. McNabb

You just can't beat the X-Men. Val Semeiks' Demon cover **[above]** learned that the hard way, as it was scrapped for a Wolverine-centric cover. Our go-to guy Bart Sears was swamped with work and had hit a wall trying to come up with a concept.

Asking for suggestions, then-Creative Director Pat McCallum sketched this out and faxed it over to Sears. The final result—a visceral Wolverine vs. Sabretooth duel—remains one of *Wizard*'s all-time fan-favorites.

XIMUM·COVERAGE

The Maxx, Julia ©

20 THE MAXX (April 1993)
PENCILER/INKER: Sam Kieth
COLORIST: Mark H. McNabb

After his first cover concept **[below]** was rejected (too much Julie, not enough Maxx on the front flap) artist Sam Kieth (and yeah, he spells it "ie") nailed the idea with his second try. Included in the package was a xeroxed page from his forthcoming Image series *The Maxx*. The page was a hit among the *Wizard* staff, circulated around the office and finally found a home thumb-tacked to a bulletin board. A day later Kieth frantically called asking if he had accidentally mailed us a page of original art from his comic which he needed to print the book. We hastily "found" what we didn't realize was original art, overnighted it back to its panicked poppa and—until this writing—never told Kieth it had been hanging next to our water cooler.

BLOOD'S YOUNG GUNS

Youngblood © & ™ 1993 Rob Liefeld

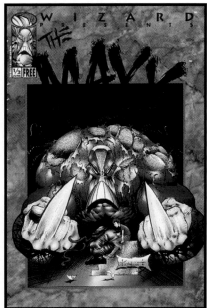

21

YOUNGBLOOD (May 1993)
PENCILER/INKER: Jae Lee
COLORIST: Mark H. McNabb

Meet one of the best-selling issues of *Wizard* ever produced. Not so much due to the editorial content or cover (from left, Youngblood's Diehard, Chapel, Shaft, Bedrock and Vogue), but because it featured the first-ever Wizard Entertainment exclusive offer: *The Maxx* #1/2 **[above]**. The tremendous fan response completely surprised and overwhelmed our customer service staff at the time. *Wizard* exclusives (#1/2 comic issues, action figures, etc.) would become the norm by issue #33.

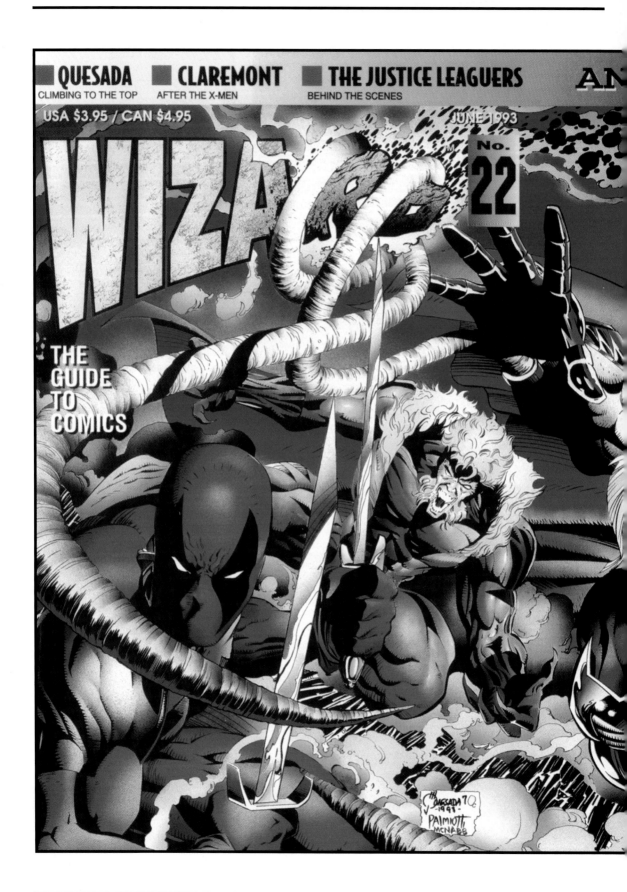

X-TREME STRUGGLE

22 X-VILLAINS (June 1993)
PENCILER: Joe Quesada
INKER: Jimmy Palmiotti
COLORIST: Mark H. McNabb

Looking for the sales power of another X-Men cover—but wanting to mix it up a little for the fans—we went with an all-X-villains image (from left: Deadpool, Sabretooth, Omega Red, Apocalypse and Stryfe), made notable by the fact that it was the first *Wizard* cover drawn by then-rookie penciler Joe Quesada.

Taking a nod from *Playboy* magazine (which hides the *Playboy* rabbit icon on every cover), we hid our own icon on the covers: cow heads. Why cow heads? Then-*Wizard* Designer Brad Fountain had created a *Wizard* ad campaign featuring spandex-clad cows in superhero settings **[below]**, and we latched onto the cow as our unofficial mascot (you can spot one of the cow heads to the left of Quesada's signature). The hidden cow-head gimmick would continue off and on for about a year before we finally realized how weird it was.

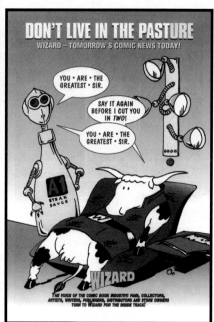

23 DEATHMATE (July 1993)

PENCILER/INKER: Bart Sears
COLORIST: Mark H. McNabb

To celebrate the Image/Valiant crossover event *Deathmate*, we went for *Wizard*'s first *triple*-gatefold cover and showcased the respective companies' heavy hitters (from left: Solar vs. Supreme, Bloodshot vs. Diehard, Void vs. X-O and Ripclaw vs. Turok).

By this time, cover artist Bart Sears could have fun signing his real name to *Wizard* covers, here penning it as "Sears?"

Not being able to complete this massive cover in time for our advance advertisements, Sears turned around this promotional pic **[bottom right]** to get fans juiced. Bart Sears: King of Men.

EATH DO US PART.

24 **BATMAN** (August 1993)
PENCILER: Joe Quesada
INKER: Jimmy Palmiotti
COLORIST: Mark H. McNabb

DC Comics felt this cover (featuring Robin, Azrael and the new armored Batman vs. Bane) gave away too much of the mystery surrounding Batman's new look. We had the Batman figure re-inked to conceal Batman, and the original, uncensored art **[top right]** wouldn't see print until used as interior art in *Wizard* #25.

To help build buzz for the issue, Quesada and Palmiotti created a second piece of art **[bottom right]** for ad purposes to tease the new Batman design.

EBORN!

RRRRGGH!!!!!!"

25 DEATHBLOW
(September 1993)
PENCILER/INKER: Jim Lee
COLORIST: Mark H. McNabb

Our 25th issue anniversary. Are 25 issues *really* an anniversary? Whatever. We celebrated with a Deathblow cover by one of the hottest artists in the biz. To help us promote the event, Lee drew us a secondary piece to use in hyping the issue in advertisements **[below]**.

■ LARRY STROMAN
LIFE AFTER IMAGE

■ SPIDEY STAFFERS
BAGLEY, MICHELINIE, AND CO.

■ CARD GUIDE
NON-SPORTS CARDS

"TRICK O

USA $3.95 / CAN $4.95

OCTOBER 1993

WIZARD

No. 26

THE
GUIDE
TO
COMICS

26 **SPIDER-MAN** (October 1993)
PENCILER: Mark Bagley
INKER: Larry Mahlstedt
COLORIST: Mark H. McNabb

Using a gimmick that didn't work the first time (*Wizard* #6's
Hulk variants), we had artist Mark Bagley draw two versions
of this cover: Spidey vs. the Hobgoblin (who was hot at the
time) and Spidey vs. the Green Goblin (who was dead at the
time). Ten percent of all copies shipped were the Green
Goblin cover…that no one noticed **[top right]**. *Sigh.*

Bagley, who was still under the impression we incorporated the *Wizard* cap motif, drew the pair of Goblins with
the *Wizard* star pattern on their caps and robes **[bottom
right]**. We asked the colorist to discard the stars.

SPIDER-MAN, HOBGOBLIN ™ & © 1993 MARVEL ENTERTAINMENT GROUP, INC.

LARRY STROMAN
LIFE AFTER IMAGE

SPIDEY STAFFERS
BAGLEY, MICHELINIE, AND CO.

CARD GUIDE
NON-SPORTS CARDS

"TRICK OR TREAT?"

USA $3.95 / CAN $4.95

OCTOBER 1993

WIZARD No. 26

THE GUIDE TO COMICS

SPIDER-MAN, GREEN GOBLIN ™ & © 1993 MARVEL ENTERTAINMENT GROUP, INC.

27 **WILDC.A.T.S** (November 1993)
PENCILER: Jim Lee
INKER: Scott Williams
COLORIST: Digital Chameleon

Originally slated as a Maverick vs. Omega Red cover by
Mark Texeira **[top right]**, the waning popularity of those
characters had us switch gears and turn to Jim Lee, mark-
ing his fourth *Wizard* cover. The WildC.A.T.s (from left:
Spartan, Void, Grifter, Maul, Warblade, Voodoo, Emp and
Zealot) would snag a cover for the second time.

This also has the distinction for being our first com-
puter-colored cover, which at the time was a fairly new
technology used mostly on Image comic titles.

28 **THE SIMPSONS** (December 1993)
PENCILERS/INKERS/COLORISTS: Steve Vance and
Bill Morrison

What started out as a Bart Simpson single panel cover
grew into a rare triple gatefold when we told the folks
over at Bongo Comics to "go nuts" with not only who they
put on the cover, but how many characters they could use.
The final tally: Bartman, Radioactive Man, Fallout Boy,
Homer, Maggie, Marge, Lisa, Kent Brockman, Dr. Marvin
Monroe, Lou, Eddie and Chief Wiggum. Twelve characters
set an impressive *Wizard* cover record, and one that
would last…three issues.

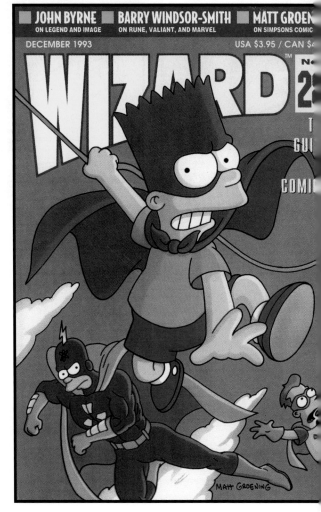

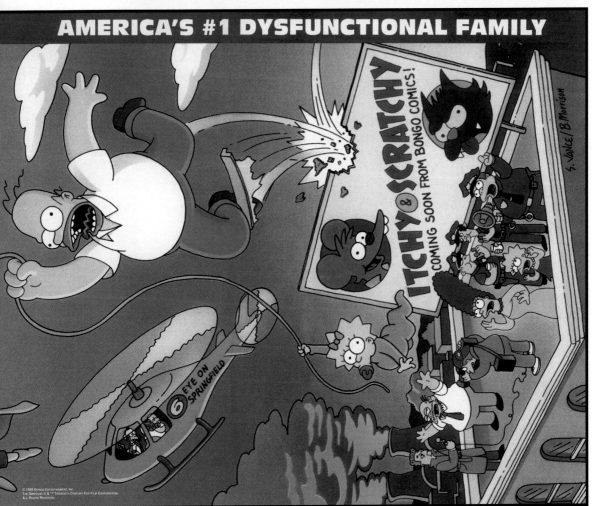

300 PAGE YEAR-END SPECTACULAR!

JANUARY 1994   USA $4.95 / CAN $5.95

WIZARD™ No. 29

THE
GUIDE
TO
COMICS

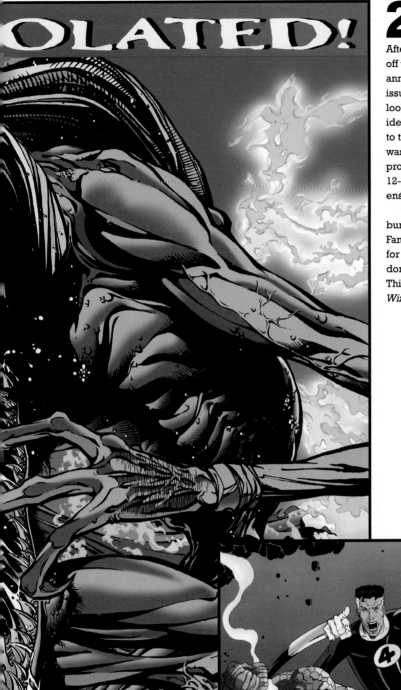

29 **SPAWN** (January 1994)
PENCILER/INKER: Bart Sears
COLORIST: Digital Chameleon

After the success of issue #25, we kicked
off what we'd hoped would become an
annual event for our December-shipping
issue. We created a 300-page "Year Ender,"
looking back on the year that was. The
idea proved wildly popular and continues
to this day, but this first "Year Ender"
wasn't greenlit until the beginning of its
production cycle, forcing the staff to work
12-hour days, seven days a week to
ensure the issue shipped on time.

To help give the issue some heat, we
bumped the original cover for the issue—a
Fantastic Four cover by Ron Lim **[below]**—
for Spawn (taking on Violator), who
dominated the sales charts at the time.
This would mark Bart Sears' six billionth
Wizard cover.

30 BEAVIS AND BUTT-HEAD (February 1994)
PENCILER/INKER: Kevin Cofton
COLORIST: Digital Chameleon

The original version of the cover **[bottom right]** featured a riff on the then-headline grabbing Death of Superman storyline, but MTV and DC Comics couldn't see eye-to-eye on the image at the time and it was pulled. The second draft featured Beavis & Butthead daydreaming away on a couch **[top right]**, but we flipped the image as to showcase the more-recognizable depictions of the characters on the front flap.

This issue also represents our first design overhaul, where we not only streamlined the cover design somewhat (note the placement of the issue number), but also mucked with the interior design as well.

31a LEGEND (March 1994)
PENCILERS/INKERS: Art Adams, John Byrne, Paul Chadwick, Geof Darrow, Dave Gibbons, Mike Mignola and Frank Miller

COLORIST: Digital Chameleon

Our first Dark Horse cover, our first cover with text blurbs printed on the actual cover (which would become the norm with issue #101), a rare triple gatefold cover and—at 19—the new record for characters on a cover. Ready? Here goes (from left): Marv, Hellboy, Martha Washington, the Surgeon General, Belabet, The Torch of Liberty, Hardbody, Sprint, Goldie, Wendy, Doc Danger, Monkeyman, O'Brien, Dwight, Rusty, Big Guy, Bounce, Concrete and The Shrewmanoid. This record would hold until issue #83.

When Dark Horse announced its new Legend imprint, we asked John Byrne to compose the jam cover. Each Legend artist did their artwork separately, then Byrne pasted all the photo-statted art together onto a single illustration board. He literally pleaded with us not to use the "air-brushed-until-it-begs-for-mercy" coloring, and also requested a white background—another first for *Wizard*.

31b LOBO (March 1994)
PAINTER: Glenn Fabry

Some last minute juggling accommodated the ads behind the triple gate and single-panel covers of #31. The Lobo cover was originally a gatefold featuring the Demon [opposite, bottom left], but was pared down to a single panel due to the character's waning popularity.

32 SPAWN AND BATMAN (April 1994)
PENCILERS/INKERS: Todd McFarlane and Frank Miller

COLORIST: Digital Chameleon

Todd McFarlane called late into #32's production run and offered us a Spawn/Batman jam cover, and the topical power of that project bumped the planned Catwoman cover until next issue [see page 52]. The final jam piece not only featured a comical snafu (...how many moons?), but layout dictated that we do something we'd never done before: print all cover text—logo included—on the clear polybag.

wizard big covers book

...the cat's meow!

33 CATWOMAN (May 1994)
PENCILER/INKER: Jim Balent
COLORIST: Digital Chameleon

Bumped from *Wizard* #32, this Catwoman image originally tied into that issue's Scavenger Hunt, where we asked fans to mail us obscure stuff and answer weird answers. The gimmick: have the fans count the myriad number of cats on the cover (57 of the lil' critters total).

We had Balent—in a nod to Catwoman's character—toss an issue of *Wizard* with Batman on the cover (issue #4) in the garbage. He agreed, but only if we cleared it with the artist who drew that cover: Bart Sears. We gave him Wittman's phone number instead.

During the printing of the issue, the foreman at the plant worriedly called our head honcho Gareb Shamus and asked if he had okayed "the issue of *Wizard* with the naked purple chick on the cover." After explaining how costumes—and gravity—work in comics, the issue printed and shipped.

E X-MEN'S BETTER HALF.

JEAN GREY, POLARIS, PSYLOCKE, ROGUE, AND STORM ™ & © 1994 MARVEL ENTERTAINMENT GROUP.
BONE ™ & © 1994 JEFF SMITH

34 X-WOMEN (June 1994)
PENCILER/INKER: Jim Balent
COLORIST: Digital Chameleon

So what bumps a *Wizard* X-Men cover? A different X-Men cover. Riding the momentum of Jim Balent's white-hot bad girl art, Darick Robertson's Sabretooth/X-Men cover **[below]** got the boot in favor of this cheesecake shot of X-ladies (from left) Psylocke, Rogue, Jean Grey, Polaris and Storm. And no, we don't recall how Polaris snuck onto this cover.

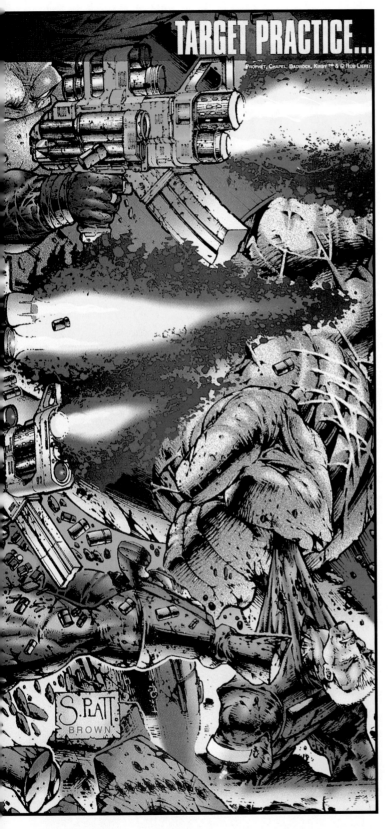

PROPHET (July 1994)
PENCILER/INKER: Stephen Platt
COLORIST: Digital Chameleon

35a

Still enamored with the "count the cats" contest idea that almost ran with *Wizard* #33's Catwoman cover, we applied it to this cover (clockwise from left: Prophet, Chapel, Badrock and Kirby) with a "count the shell casings" spin. When we contacted artist Stephen Platt to see how many he had drawn into the piece, his delayed answer was a simple "...dude." After a dozen tries with a dozen different answers, we stopped counting, and the contest never ran.

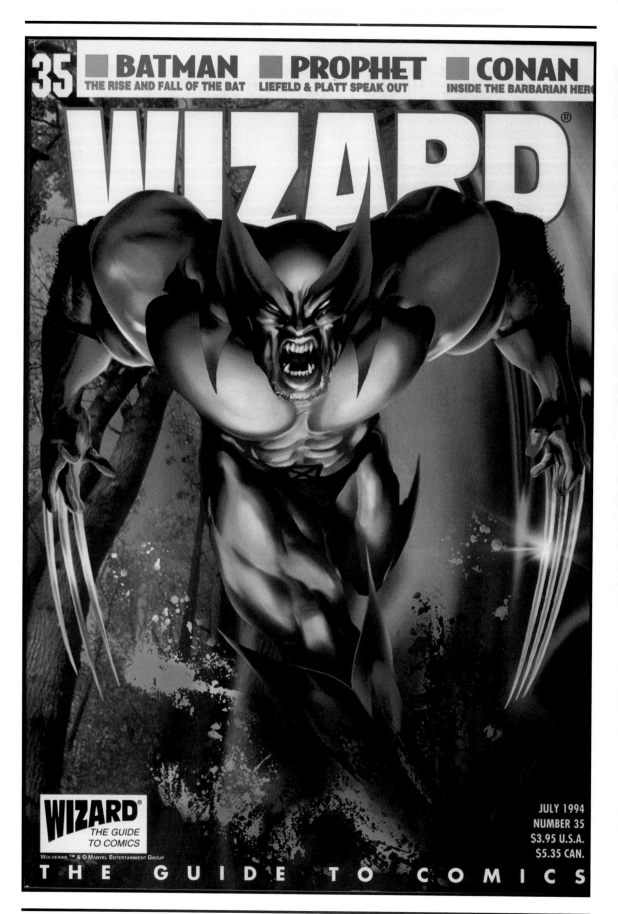

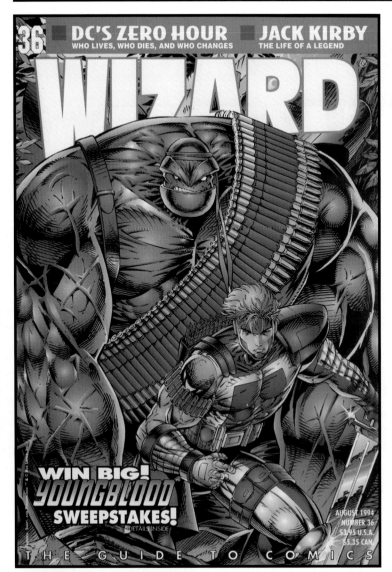

35b
WOLVERINE (July 1994)
ART: Fleer Flair based on art by Mark Texeira

The Fleer trading card company—a subsidiary of Marvel—produced an extremely popular line of Marvel-character-based cards called "Fleer Flair," which used computer coloring to paint over existing inked artwork. (In fact, Marvel still uses that style to color the covers to *Ultimate Spider-Man*.) This cover—also used as trading card art—originally appeared as inked art on the cover to *Wolverine* #67.

36a
YOUNGBLOOD (August 1994)
PENCILER: Rob Liefeld
INKER: Danny Miki
COLORIST: Extreme Studios

After taking a short sabbatical from comics, artist Rob Liefeld busily planned his triumphant return. While we already had a Youngblood cover planned for the next issue to tie into the hoopla, Liefeld called at the last minute and pushed hard to get a Badrock/Shaft cover on this issue, as well. It ended up running, and put the kibosh on artist John Byrne's Next Men cover **[top right]** we had originally planned to use.

IN DEEP...

THE LIZARD, SPIDER-MAN, CARNAGE, VENOM, DOCTOR OCTOPUS, THE HOBGOBLIN ™ & © MARVEL ENTERTAINMENT GROUP, INC.

36b SPIDER-MAN VS. ROGUES GALLERY (August 1994)

PENCILER: Joe Quesada
INKER: Jimmy Palmiotti
COLORIST: Digital Chameleon

When artist Joe Quesada completed the cover (featuring the web-head vs. the Lizard, Carnage, Hobgoblin, Dr. Octopus and Venom), he and collaborator Jimmy Palmiotti hand-delivered the piece to tell us they were breaking away from their home at Valiant Comics to create their own company, Event Comics. Then the pair pulled a second piece of artwork from a folder, this one featuring Event characters Ash, Kid Death and Fluffy. They wanted to debut the characters on a *Wizard* cover, and do it in a way that had never been done before. This would lead to two firsts for *Wizard* #37.

Incidentally, that little black and white kitty on the windowsill casually observing the chaos? That's Quesada's own cat, White Sox.

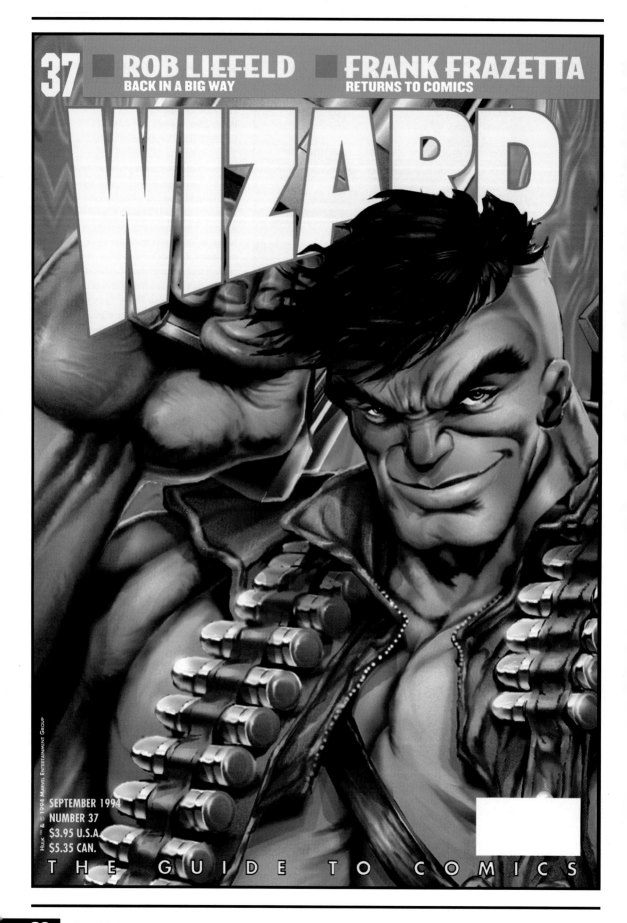

■ **JOE QUESADA** UNVEILS EVENT COMICS   ■ **FRANK FRAZETTA** RETURNS TO COMICS

WIZARD

SEPTEMBER 1994
NUMBER 37
$3.95 U.S.A.
$5.35 CAN.

THE   GUIDE   TO   COMICS

37a

HULK (September 1994)
ART: Fleer Flair, based on art by Dale Keown and Mark Farmer
Why does the Hulk need a gun? Either way, this art originally appeared as interior art in *Incredible Hulk* #391.

37b

ASH AND KID DEATH (September 1994)
PENCILER: Joe Quesada
INKER: Jimmy Palmiotti
COLORIST: Simon Erich

When artists Joe Quesada and Jimmy Palmiotti wanted to debut the launch of their creator-owned Event Comics line through *Wizard*, they pushed hard for a cover. And they got it, although we had already agreed to Hulk and Youngblood (see next page) covers. The addition of the Event cover pushed us to an unprecedented third cover variant. To further make the Event cover stand out, Quesada and Palmiotti had created it as a sideways "fold down," with all cover elements presented vertically instead of horizontally, something *Wizard* had never done before or since.

YOUNGBLOOD '94

YOUNGBLOOD 'TM & © 1994 ROB LIEFELD IN

37c

YOUNGBLOOD
(September 1994)
PENCILER: Rob Liefeld

INKER: Dan Panosian
COLORIST: Extreme Studios

Back-to-back covers featuring the same characters, a stunt that had never been pulled off until Rob Liefeld made it happen. *Wizard* #36 featured his Youngblood characters, as did this issue's cover with Badrock, Diehard and Troll. This marks the seventh time Liefeld's Image characters would appear on our cover (including issue #10, #16, #21, #23, #35 and #36), all of which occurred in three years' time. It's a testament to Liefeld's aggressive promotion of his comics, something which was instrumental in making him one of the most successful comic book personalities of the early to mid-1990s.

...CLAWS AND EFFECT

38 WOLVERINE
(October 1994)
PENCILERS: Adam and Andy Kubert
INKER: Matthew Ryan
COLORIST: Digital Chameleon

A Kubert brothers collaboration: Adam—at that time the artist on Marvel's *Wolverine* series—penciled Wolvie, while Andy—then-artist on *X-Men*—penciled Sabretooth. The first *Wizard* cover for either brother, it would mark the fourth cover for Wolverine, who needed a haircut. Unfortunately, it meant bumping yet another cover—this one by Tom Grummett and Karl Kesel featuring Robin, Superboy, Azrael-Batman and Superman **[below]**, hot off of their mega-popular "Knightfall" and "Death/Return of Superman" story arcs.

...SPEAR FISHING

SPAWN AND ANGELA ARE REGISTERED TRADEMARKS OF TODD MCFARLANE PRODUCTIONS INC.

39 SPAWN VS. ANGELA
(November 1994)
PENCILER/INKER: Greg Capullo
COLORIST: Digital Chameleon

First *Wizard* cover by Greg Capullo, who had just accepted the unenviable task of following artist Todd McFarlane on *Spawn*. Needless to say, he quickly attracted a strong fan following. Once we saw the dynamic style and in-your-face composition of the sketches for this cover, we immediately assigned him the cover to the following month's issue of *Wizard*.

...TRICK OR TREAT!

40a

VIOLATOR
(December 1994)
PENCILER/INKER: Greg Capullo
COLORIST: I.H.O.C.

One of the more involved, clever and just-plain fun gatefold compositions to date. We asked Capullo to give us something special for the cover of this—our first Halloween-themed issue—and he handed in one of our all-time favorite pieces. Once you get past the feral monstrosities lunging at you, check out the evil fun the Violator brothers [from left, Vandalizer, Vacillator, Violator, Vaporizer and Vindicator] are having with the hapless trick-or-treaters. Note: Never give demons candy corn.

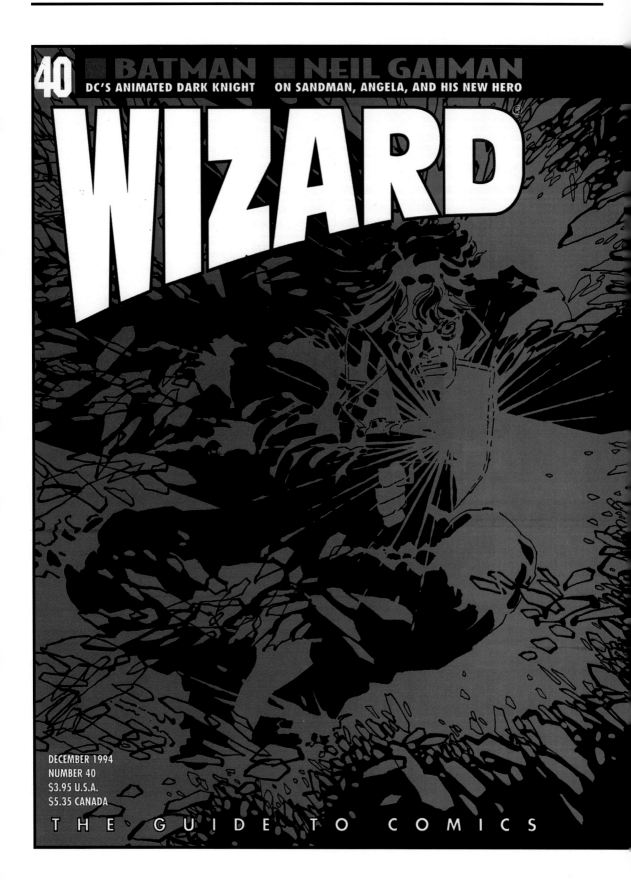

40 ■ **BATMAN** ■ **NEIL GAIMAN**

DC'S ANIMATED DARK KNIGHT   ON SANDMAN, ANGELA, AND HIS NEW HERO

WIZARD ®

DECEMBER 1994
NUMBER 40
$3.95 U.S.A.
$5.35 CANADA

THE GUIDE TO COMICS

...EAT HOT LEAD!!!!

SIN CITY ™ & © 1994 FRANK MILLER. ALL RIGHTS RES[

40b

SIN CITY'S DWIGHT
(December 1994)
PENCILER/INKER: Frank Miller

COLORIST: N/A

When we approached artist Frank Miller to do a cover, he agreed on one condition: the art would be colored in the monochromatic style of his *Sin City* series, breaking *Wizard*'s tradition of full-color covers. An event that would only happen one other time, coincidentally enough with another Sin City cover by Miller, issue #73.

300-PAGE YEAR-END SPECTACULAR!

WIZARD ®

JANUARY 1995
NUMBER 41
$4.95 U.S.A.
S6.75 CANADA

THE GUIDE TO COMICS

Gambit ™ & © Marvel Entertainment Group.

0 09281 02725 6   01

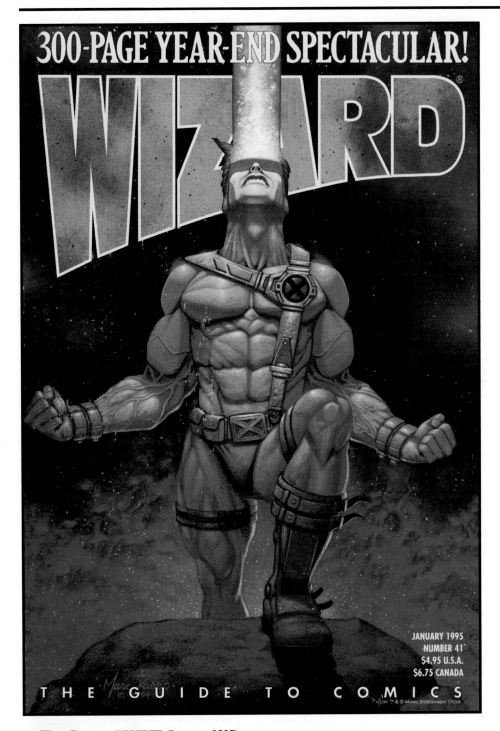

41a **GAMBIT** (January 1995)
PAINTER: Ray Lago
The one-two punch of a 300-page *Wizard* Year-End special issue coupled with dynamic X-Men covers made for a blockbuster sales issue. It sold so well that *Wizard*'s Circulation Manager at the time wanted to rerun the covers the following year (and no, don't flip ahead to check…we didn't run 'em again).

41b **CYCLOPS** (January 1995)
PAINTER: Marc Sasso
Tightest. Shirt. Ever.

42a

SILVER AGE MARVEL VILLAINS (February 1995)
PAINTER: Alex Ross

Alex Ross' amazingly photo-realistic painting style in 1993-94's *Marvels* blew us all away. So much that we asked him to create a gatefold cover with the Silver Age villains we wanted to see more of (which originally ended a little past the Red Skull's left eye). Featuring (from left) Magneto, Green Goblin, Dr. Doom, Galactus, Loki and the Red Skull, it was intended as the only cover to *Wizard* #42. But after seeing the final artwork, *Wizard* head honcho Gareb Shamus and Editor-in-Chief Pat McCallum wanted to make this cover more of an event to up the ante. They first thought to do a mirror-image version featuring the Silver Age heroes, which quickly escalated to "Let's make 'em both triple gatefolds!" Now we just had to convince Ross—then a hot up-and-comer—to not only go back and touch up the existing villains cover (adding from left of the Red Skull: the Mandarin, Mephisto, the Kingpin, Dormammu and Dr. Octopus' arms), but to create an all-new triple-gatefold piece of art—all within an impossible looming deadline. McCallum lost the coin toss to make the call...

42b SILVER AGE MARVEL HEROES (February 1995)
PENCILER: Alex Ross

...a call that would wake the artist out of bed. Not off to a great start, the idea of the Silver Age heroes cover was pitched with (clockwise from left: Hulk, Angel, Human Torch, Daredevil, Giant Man, Iceman, Cyclops, Dr, Strange, Wasp, Marvel Girl, Beast, Thor, Invisible Girl, Mr. Fantastic, Iron Man, Captain America, Spider-Man and the Thing). Ross woke up immediately—he loved the concept. Then we explained how we wanted it to be triple gatefold, which he thought was cool. Then we asked if he could go back in and add a third panel to the villains cover. Silence. At first reluctant to go back in and expand a finished piece—especially one that was laid out as a gatefold—the fan inside of Ross got the better of him. After thinking aloud the list of villains he couldn't fit on the initial gatefold that he could fit on this new panel, he agreed. The end result: what many consider the two best *Wizard* covers to ever see print. Thank you, Dormammu.

THE GUIDE TO COMICS·43   STAR TREK COMICS CLASSIC, NEXT GENERATION, & VOYAGER

WIZARD

MARCH 1995
$3.95 USA $5.35 CANADA

43 WARBLADE AND RIPCLAW (March 1995)

PENCILER: Scott Clark

INKER: Sal Regla

COLORIST: Wildstorm

A tie-in to Image Comics' *Warblade: Endangered Species* crossover mini-series, starring WildC.A.T.s' Warblade (top) and Cyberforce's Ripclaw.

WARBLADE ™ & © Aegis Entertainment, Inc. RIPCLAW ™ & © Top Cow Productions, Inc.

44

GEN 13 (April 1995)
PENCILER: J. Scott Campbell
INKER: Alex Garner
COLORIST: Wildstorm

The first J. Scott Campbell cover.

Campbell had come up with the idea of putting *Wizard* Big Cheese Gareb Shamus on the cover, but Gareb—feeling the space was better served with comic book characters—was hesitant. After seeing the artwork and finding the whole "*Wizard* Cover Photoshoot" idea clever (posing clockwise from top: Fairchild, Rainmaker and Freefall; offset from left: Gareb, security guy, Burnout, Grunge and Lynch), Gareb gave it the thumbs up, but never put his image on a cover again.

THE GUIDE TO COMICS • 45   THE COMIC INDUSTRY: **JIM SHOOTER** SHOOTS FROM THE HIP

WIZARD®

SIL VES TRI

05

0 73361 64959 1

$3.99 USA **MAY 1995** $5.40 CANADA

45a

CYBERFORCE
(May 1995)

PENCILER: Marc Silvestri
INKER: Billy Tan
COLORIST: Tyson Wengler

Our first Marc Silvestri cover, featuring Cyberforce members (from left) Cyblade, Ripclaw, Impact, Velocity, Stryker and Heatwave.

WIZARD ®

$3.99 USA **MAY 1995** $5.40 CANADA

THE GUIDE TO COMICS · 46 SELF-PUBLISHING COMICS LEARN HOW TO DO IT RIGHT

WIZARD®

$3.99 USA JUNE 1995 $5.40 CANADA

0 73361 64959 1   06

45b **CAPTAIN AMERICA** (May 1995)
ART: Fleer Flair
Hard to believe, despite the character's popularity and longevity, but this was the first Captain America solo cover and only the second time the character had appeared on a cover (see #42b).

The art was taken from the Fleer Flair trading card set.

46 **BATMAN, ROBIN AND AZRAEL** (June 1995)
PENCILER/INKER: Tom Grummett
COLORIST: I.H.O.C.
This cover—featuring supporting cast members Robin and the then-red-hot Azrael—also sported the newly designed Batman costume, which featured darker colors and the loss of his "underwear on the outside" look. Here, Batman makes a muscle. *¡Bat-macho!*

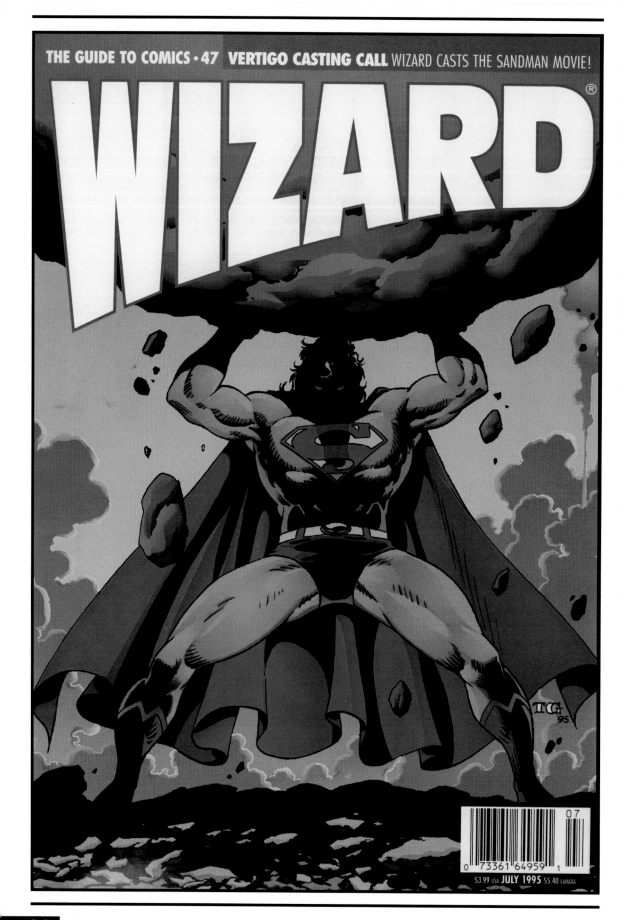

THE GUIDE TO COMICS •47 VERTIGO CASTING CALL WIZARD CASTS THE SANDMAN MOVIE!

WIZARD

$3.99 USA JULY 1995 $5.40 CANADA

0 73361 64959 1

07

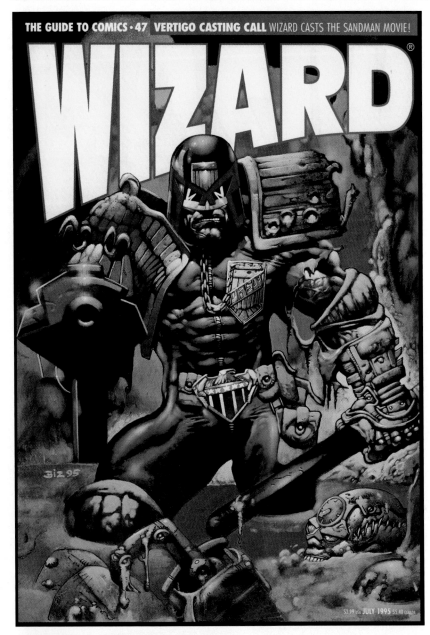

THE GUIDE TO COMICS · 47 VERTIGO CASTING CALL WIZARD CASTS THE SANDMAN MOVIE!

WIZARD

$3.99 US JULY 1995 $5.40 CANADA

47a
SUPERMAN (July 1995)
PENCILER/INKER: Tom Grummett
COLORIST: I.H.O.C.

Hard to believe, but this is the first time in the then-four-year run of *Wizard* that Superman—the most recognizable superhero on the planet—appeared on the cover (he had come close with *Wizard* #8).

Further heaping indignation on the Man of Steel, note how we approved art that features a cover no-no: the character's face is concealed in shadow (successful covers normally show characters brightly lit and easily recognizable).

Wizard Entertainment: a subsidiary of LexCorp.

47b
JUDGE DREDD (July 1995)
PAINTER: Simon Bisley

We'd been after artist Simon Bisley to do us a cover since issue #1, and we finally snagged him with this Judge Dredd shot. We're pretty sure more people saw this cover than the "Judge Dredd" movie it was tied into.

48 CATWOMAN
(August 1995)
PENCILER/INKER:

Jim Balent
COLORIST: I.H.O.C.
The return of "...that naked purple chick" (see *Wizard* #33). This time around we have Catwoman on the run after stealing Wonder Woman's lasso and Supergirl's cape.

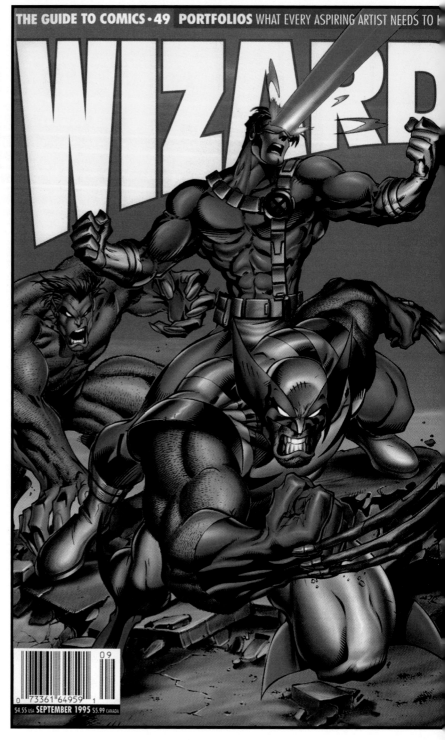

THE GUIDE TO COMICS · 49 PORTFOLIOS WHAT EVERY ASPIRING ARTIST NEEDS TO

$4.55 USA SEPTEMBER 1995 $5.99 CANADA

0 73361 64959 1

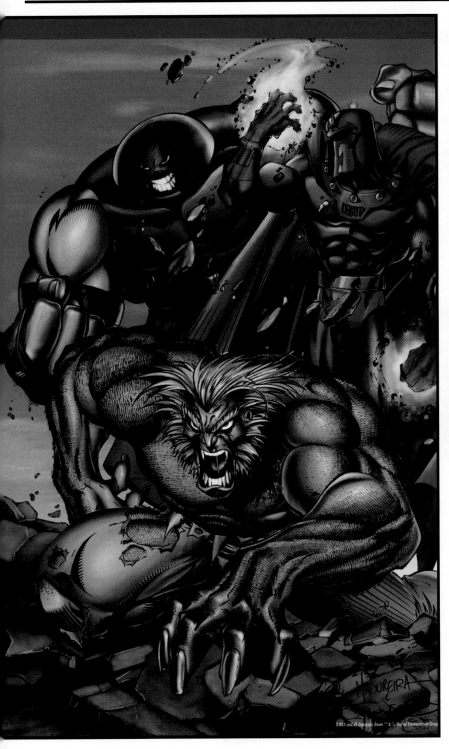

49

X-MEN
(September 1995)
PENCILER: Joe Madureira
INKER: Tim Townsend
COLORIST: Fleer

First Joe Madureira cover. The art for this cover (featuring Wolverine, Cyclops and Beast vs. Magneto, Juggernaut and Sabretooth) would later be used as art in Fleer's *Marvel OverPower* card game. It was composed in such a way that the art could later be cut down the middle and used for two separate cards **[above]**.

50 **SPIDER-MAN** (October 1995)
PENCILER/INKER: Todd McFarlane
COLORIST: Jung

For *Wizard*'s gala 50th issue, we were at a bit of a loss as to how to celebrate the event. After some back-and-forth, we repackaged and gave a new spin to the first-ever *Wizard* cover: Todd McFarlane's Spider-Man. We gave it a twist with the Fleer computer coloring.

This design would go on to influence the cover to our next anniversary issue—*Wizard* #100—as well.

51 **MAGNETO** (November 1995)
PENCILER/INKER: Andy Kubert
COLORIST: Fleer

A rare solo villain cover (from the Fleer Flair trading card line), and only the fifth in *Wizard*'s then-51 issue run (along with #9's Venom, #22's X-Villains, #40's Violator and #42's Silver Age Marvel villains). No disrespect to the Master of Magnetism, but heroes traditionally sell better on covers.

WIZARD ®

$4.55 USA **NOVEMBER 1995** $5.99 CANADA

0 25274 84070 1

MONSTERS! HOW TO CREATE THE ULTIMATE SUPERVILLAIN

WIZARD®

$4.55 USA **DECEMBER 1995** $5.99 CANADA

52a
THE PITT (December 1995)
PENCILER/INKER: DALE KEOWN
COLORIST: Olyoptics

A Halloween-themed cover and one of *Wizard*'s more humorous cover images.
Mmmm...Punisher-flavored lollipops.

52b
X-FILES (December 1995)
PAINTER: Miran Kim
An experimental cover. Normally we stress bright, spandexy-superheroes, but here we went with a darker, more abstract image featuring Agents Mulder and Scully from the "X-Files" TV show. It didn't sell as strongly as we hoped and, from then on—with some exceptions—*Wizard* would stick to superhero-specific covers.

53

SPIDER-MAN (January 1996)
PENCILER: John Romita Jr.
INKER: John Romita Sr.
COLORIST: I.H.O.C.

To help make this Year-End edition of *Wizard* more of an event, we kept it in the family by turning to legendary Spider-Man artist John Romita Sr. and his fan-favorite son John Romita Jr. to collaborate on—what else?—a Spidey cover.

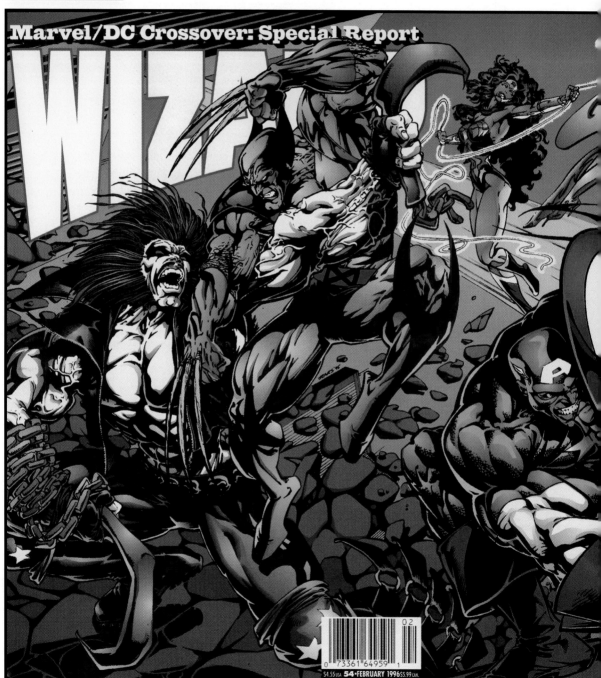

54

MARVEL VS. DC (February 1996)
PENCILER/INKER: Bart Sears
COLORIST: I.H.O.C.

We had wanted to do a Marvel vs. DC cover for years, but politics kept the crossover idea in limbo. The 1996 Marvel/DC crossover comics' event finally opened the door and we celebrated by not only bringing back the *Wizard* gatefold cover, but also by giving it a triple gate.

From left: Lobo vs. Wolverine, Wonder Woman vs. Storm, Captain America vs. Batman and Superman vs. the Hulk.

This would also mark Bart Sears' eighth *Wizard* cover, making him the most prolific *Wizard* cover artist at the time.

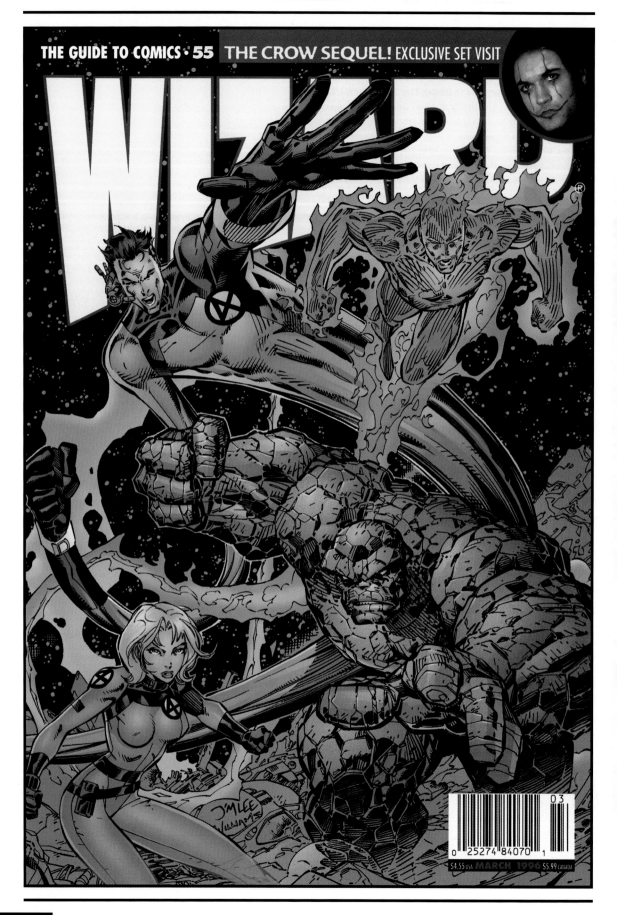

THE GUIDE TO COMICS · 55   THE CROW SEQUEL! EXCLUSIVE SET VISIT

WIZARD

$4.55 USA MARCH 1996 $5.99 CANADA

0 25274 84070 1

03

55a FANTASTIC FOUR (March 1996)

PENCILER: Jim Lee
INKER: Scott Williams
COLORIST: Homer Reyes

Originally, *Wizard* #55 featured a single cover (see #55b), but the announcement of Marvel's "Heroes Reborn" deal (where famous ex-Marvel artists relaunched core Marvel books) forced us to stop the presses, scramble to put together a story and work with Jim Lee under an impossible deadline to get a new cover created (clockwise from top left: Mr. Fantastic, the Human Torch, the Thing and Invisible Woman). The breakneck result? This cover was the first piece of finished art created as part of the "Heroes Reborn" project, debuting the event.

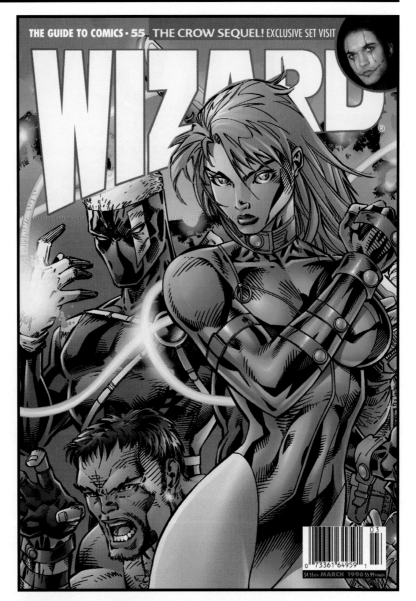

THE GUIDE TO COMICS · 55 · THE CROW SEQUEL! EXCLUSIVE SET VISIT

WIZARD

55b WILDSTORM HEROES (March 1996)

PENCILER: Jim Lee
INKER: Scott Williams
COLORIST: Tad Ehrlich

Normally when we do split covers on *Wizard*, we try to offer two distinct images by two distinct artists in an effort to appeal to the widest group of fans possible. This Lee-drawn Wildstorm cover (clockwise from top left: Backlash, Fairchild and Grunge) had already been slotted for the issue when the last minute Heroes Reborn cover was added to the mix, making this only the second time an artist produced all variant covers to one issue with all-new art for each (Alex Ross had blazed that trail with *Wizard* #42). We would try to avoid using similar artists/characters on an issue's multiple covers in the future…until, uh, next issue, that is.

THE GUIDE TO COMICS · 56   SHI! Q & A WITH **BILLY TUCCI**

WIZARD®

04
0   73361 64959   1

$4.55 USA $5.99 CAN
APRIL 1996

56a
DARK CLAW
(April 1996)
PENCILER/INKER:
Gary Frank
COLORIST: I.H.O.C

...Darkwing Duck?!? No wait, that's Dark Claw, star of Marvel and DC's jointly produced Amalgam line, which merged characters from both universes into something new. Here we see "What if Batman and Wolverine had a son?" Crazy.

56b
WOLVERINE (April 1996)
PENCILER/INKER: Bart Sears
COLORIST: Brad Perkins

Two Wolverine covers in one month. Well, sort of.

Drawn three years earlier, this cover was deemed "too violent" by Marvel. Wolverine? Violent? The cover was eventually greenlit, though the claws had to be redrawn and recolored to reflect the bone claws Wolverine was sporting at the time instead of his trademark metal pig stickers.

And those dead guys? Omega Red, Mystique, Sabretooth and the Silver Samurai.

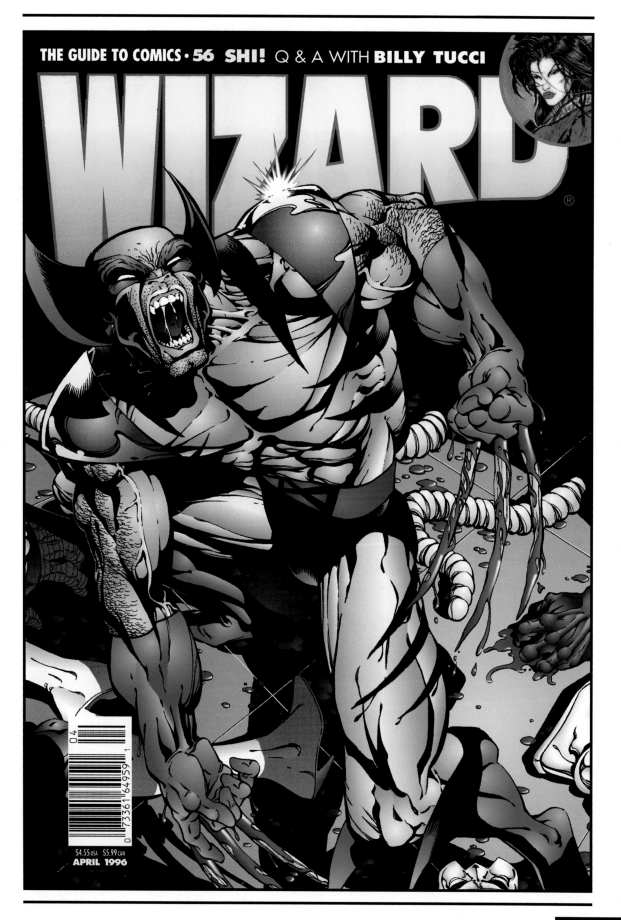

THE GUIDE TO COMICS · 57   LEE & LIEFELD UNLEASH THEIR MARVEL PLANS

WIZARD

$4.55 USA **MAY 1996** $5.99 CANADA

57a KINGDOM COME
(May 1996)
PAINTER: Alex Ross

Ross painted a five-character *Kingdom Come* piece featuring (from left) Green Lantern, Flash, Red Robin, Wonder Woman and Superman **[above]**, but we ended up chopping some characters in favor of making the big guns larger.

Note how the wings on the Flash's helmet cleverly give Red Robin the illusion of a Batman cowl.

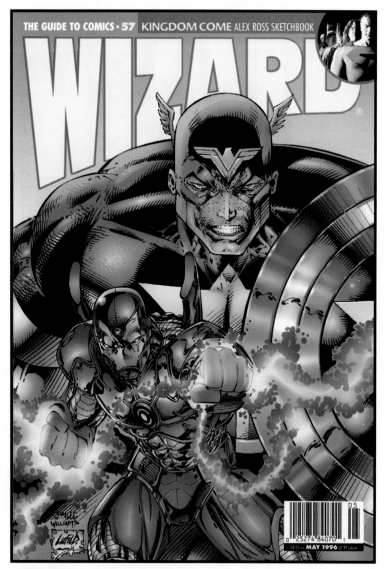

57b HEROES REBORN (May 1996)
PENCILERS: Jim Lee and Rob Liefeld
INKERS: Scott Williams and Jon Sibal
COLORISTS: Wildstorm and Extreme Studios

Jam covers: loved by our Sales Department because it can market more premier names…and hated by our Design Department because of the risks involved. These covers demand enormous amounts of time, coordination and communication in order to be successful, and this one somehow never came together. The idea was to have Captain America (drawn by Rob Liefeld) and Iron Man (drawn by Jim Lee) fighting side-by-side. Cap was drawn first by Rob Liefeld, who must have re-envisioned this image as a montage because where you see the art end on the cover is where the art ends on the original drawing. This presented a challenge for Jim Lee to fit Iron Man into the piece, but he did a bang-up job with the space he had to work with.

The final result: we wish we had more time to do this one over.

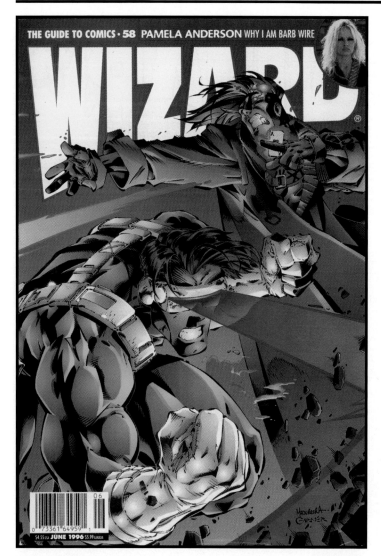

THE GUIDE TO COMICS · 58   PAMELA ANDERSON WHY I AM BARB WIRE

WIZARD

JUNE 1996

58 X-MEN (June 1996)
PENCILER: Joe Madureira
INKER: Alex Garner
COLORIST: I.H.O.C.

Wizard doesn't decide what characters grace the cover or who draws it. The fans do. Based on the individual issue sales and fan feedback, we respond accordingly. The result: X-Men. And lots of 'em. This marks our 16th cover featuring characters from Marvel's mutant team, more than any other character or team at the time.

We try to vary which X-Men characters appear on the cover in order to keep things fresh. Here, Gambit and Cyclops slaughter innocent lawn gnomes (off panel).

THE GUIDE TO COMICS · 59   SUPERMAN THE ANIMATED SERIES PREVIEWED

59a SHI (July 1996)
PENCILER: Bill Tucci
INKER: Rob Stull
COLORIST: I.H.O.C.

Another example of how *Wizard* covers moved closer to cleaner, single image shots as opposed to the "cram in as many guys as you can!" cover designs.

59b SUPERMAN (July 1996)
PENCILER: Joe Quesada
INKER: Jimmy Palmiotti
COLORIST: I.H.O.C.

We would later use this cover and the rejected sketches **[at left]** as a "How to draw a comic book cover" tutorial in our "Basic Training" how-to-draw section, hosted by artist Joe Quesada in our very next issue.

Note Superman's long hair, a temporary fashion alteration done to make the Man of Steel look like a pretentious art major.

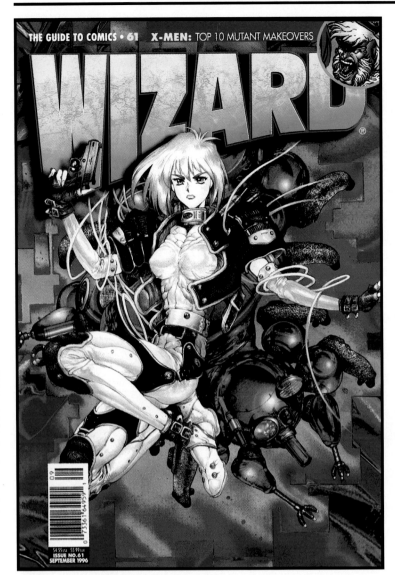

THE GUIDE TO COMICS • 61   X-MEN: TOP 10 MUTANT MAKEOVERS

WIZARD®

ISSUE NO. 61
SEPTEMBER 1996

60 **HULK** (August 1996)
PENCILER/INKER: Bart Sears
COLORIST: Twilight Graphics

Our fifth anniversary issue.

To help celebrate the event, we oversized the issue and pursued two different cover possibilities: a more celebratory cover or an interesting Captain Marvel-themed **[bottom]** gatefold cover pitched to us by Alex Ross. Ross positioned Marvel Comics' Ms. Marvel, Captain Marvel and Marvel Boy opposite DC Comics' Mary Marvel, Captain Marvel and Captain Marvel Jr. After dwelling on it, we went with this in-your-face Hulk cover instead, featuring the jade giant smashing through a wall of old *Wizard* covers. We felt it was an image more in tune with our celebratory event. The Ross cover was delayed for a later issue that sadly didn't materialized, and it never made it past the initial sketch phase.

61a **GHOST IN THE SHELL** (September 1996)
PENCILER/INKER/COLORIST: Masamune Shirow
Wizard's first anime/manga cover. Timed to coincide with Dark Horse's then-annual "Manga Month" event, and would mark *Wizard*'s first tentative testing of the waters that would lead us to launch our own anime/manga magazine *Anime Insider* several years later.

MS. MARVEL   CAPTAIN MARVEL MARVEL BOY   MARY MARVEL   CAPTAIN MARVEL CAPTAIN MARVEL JR.

61b X-MEN (September 1996)
PENCILER/INKER: Bart Sears (drawing as Wittman)
COLORIST: Twilight Graphics

From looking at the initial sketch for the cover **[top right]** to the final design, you can see how the change of a simple gesture can alter the feel of a piece. The initial sketch has Sabretooth missing his swing ("D'OH!"), while in the final version he's rearing back for what looks to be a monstrous swipe at Psylocke.

62 SPIDER-MAN AND SPAWN (October 1996)
PENCILER: J. Scott Campbell
INKER: Tim Townsend
COLORIST: Twilight Graphics

Fans clamored for the return of Todd McFarlane to the character that made him famous: Spider-Man. While McFarlane—busy building his Spawn franchise—had no such plans and opted not to do a Spawn/Spidey crossover cover, we pursued the idea. Thankfully, fan-favorite J. Scott Campbell jumped at the chance and sketched a fight scene **[bottom right]** and a comin' atcha pose, which we went with. Campbell even penciled promo art for our ads **[middle right]**. The event—which we touted as a "guaranteed no-brainer"—has yet to arrive seven years later. Sigh. Let's move on...

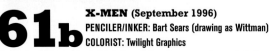

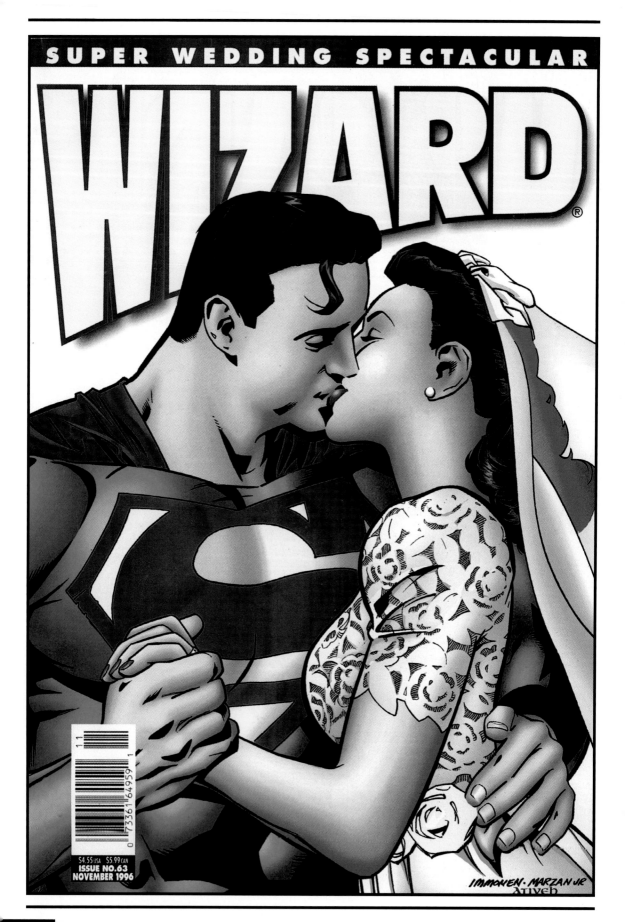

63a

SUPERMAN AND LOIS LANE (November 1996)

PENCILER: Stuart Immonen
INKER: Jose Marzan Jr.
COLORIST: Twilight Graphics

We bumped the issue's existing JLA cover by Bart Sears **[directly below]**, and ran the popular Superman wedding cover.

Note the initial sketch for the piece **[bottom]**. It originally had Lois on the left, but when magazines are racked they're occasionally laid one atop the other, with only the far left of the cover showing. That means your cover better have something enticing or recognizable—like Supes' famous "S" shield—in the limelight.

HALLOWEEN SPECIAL ISSUE

WIZARD

ISSUE NO. 63
NOVEMBER 1996

$4.55 US $5.99 CAN

63b

WITCHBLADE AND DARKNESS (November 1996)

PENCILER: Michael Turner/Marc Silvestri
INKER: D-Tron/Batt
COLORIST: J.D. Smith/Steve Firchow

Who scored a *Wizard* cover first: Witchblade or the Darkness? The answer: it's a tie. Toss in how this is also Michael Turner's first *Wizard* cover, and you have a giant pile of goodness. And cleavage. Next!

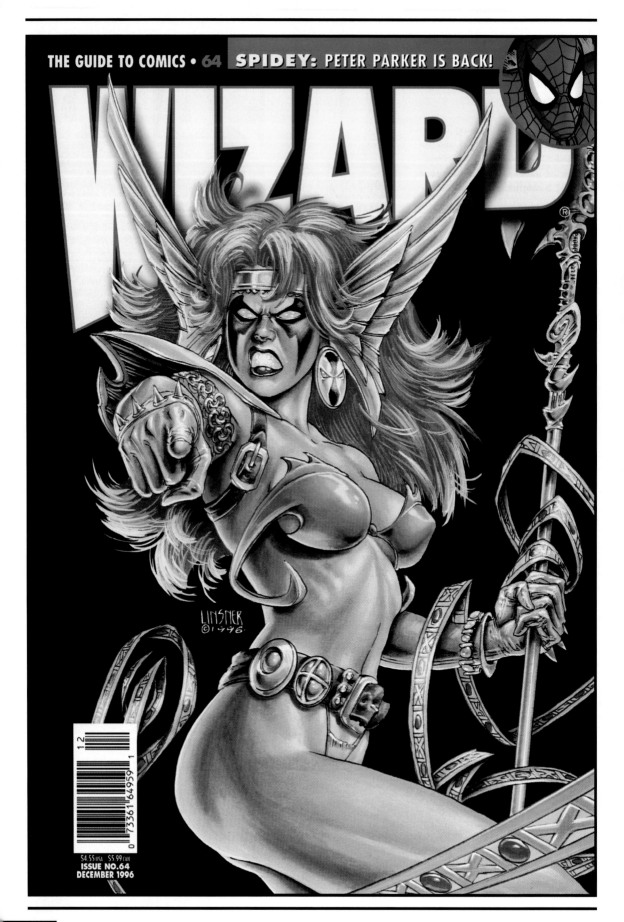

64a ANGELA
(December 1996)
PAINTER: Joseph Michael Linsner

Joseph Michael Linser's first *Wizard* cover. Note how the near full-body final cover evolved from the initial close-up sketches **[below]**.

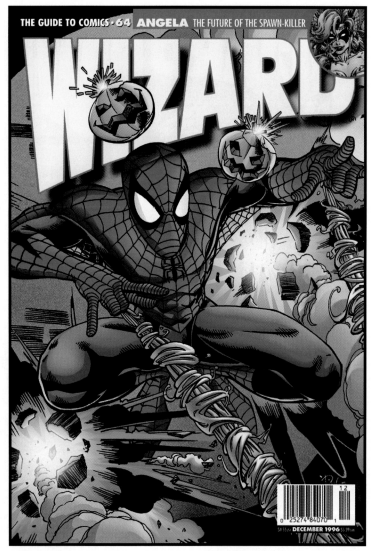

64b SPIDER-MAN
(December 1996)
PENCILER: Mike Wieringo

INKER: Richard Case
COLORIST: Twilight Graphics

What started out as a Spider-Man vs. Hobgoblin cover where both combatants were visible **[at right]**, would evolve—via 13 different sketches—into a solo Spidey battling an off-screen 'Goblin.

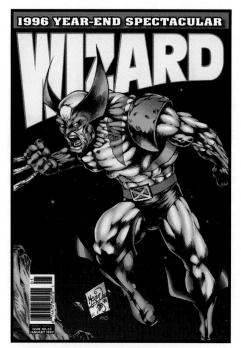

1996 YEAR-END SPECTACULAR

WIZARD

65 WOLVERINE (January 1997)
PENCILER/INKER: Kevin Lau
COLORIST: Twilight Graphics

Another Year-End edition. We originally ran down a list of opponents for Wolverine to be fighting on this cover (ranging from Sabretooth to Spider-Man to Batman), but in the end pushed forward with a single, dominant character.

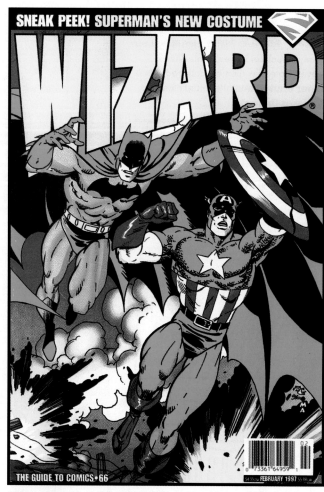

SNEAK PEEK! SUPERMAN'S NEW COSTUME

WIZARD

THE GUIDE TO COMICS • 66

FEBRUARY 1997

66a BATMAN AND CAPTAIN AMERICA
(February 1997)
PENCILER/INKER: Tom Grummett
COLORIST: Twilight Graphics

The friendlier climate between longtime comic rivals Marvel Entertainment and DC Comics made crossover covers—once a political sticking point—something the companies allowed, particularly because there was a Captain America/Batman crossover comic out that month. Here we see both heroes moments before exploding.

66b GEN 13 (February 1997)
PENCILER: J. Scott Campbell
INKER: Alex Garner
COLORIST: Wildstorm

J. Scott Campbell: king of thumbnail sketches **[left]**. Wanting to do something fun with the Gen 13 cover (from left: Rainmaker, Burnout, Freefall, Fairchild and Grunge), Campbell sent over nearly a dozen sketches with various cover treatments. We call this one "Fairchild bends waaaaaay over."

'97 TOY PREVIEW! JEDI & X-MEN MONSTERS!

WIZARD

$4.55 USA **MARCH 1997** $5.99 CAN

THE GUIDE TO COMICS•67

67a
HEROES REBORN
(March 1997)
PENCILER: Jim Lee
INKER: Tom McWeeney
COLORIST: Wildstorm Colors/Twilight Graphics

With "Heroes Reborn" setting the comic biz on fire, we'd be nuts not to ask artist Jim Lee to do another cover, but we couldn't decide which characters to use: the Fantastic Four or Iron Man. We settled for Iron Man and a more dynamic looking FF member, the Thing (who beat out the Human Torch mostly because his color scheme was too close to Iron Man's).

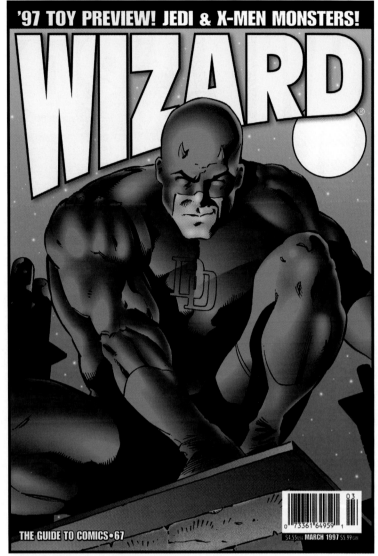

'97 TOY PREVIEW! JEDI & X-MEN MONSTERS!

WIZARD

THE GUIDE TO COMICS • 67

$4.55 USA **MARCH 1997** $5.99 CAN

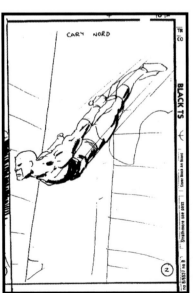

67b
DAREDEVIL (March 1997)
PENCILER: Cary Nord
INKER: Matthew Ryan
COLORIST: Twilight Graphics

While Daredevil has emerged as one of Marvel's more high-profile characters, that wasn't always the case. Long before the hit movie, Brian Michael Bendis' acclaimed run or the hugely successful Marvel Knights relaunch, DD snagged his first solo *Wizard* cover ever (and his second appearance after his cameo shot on #42b's cover) thanks to the cult favorite run of creators Karl Kesel and Cary Nord. We were impressed with Nord's sketches **[middle and bottom left]** where he tested different poses and angles, but we felt the final cover image was strongest because it showed DD's face and chest emblem amid a spooky rooftop setting.

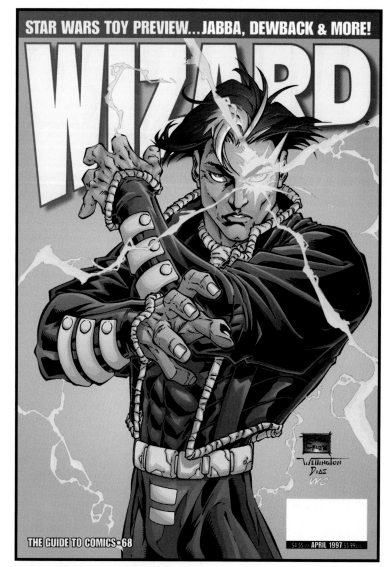

STAR WARS TOY PREVIEW...JABBA, DEWBACK & MORE!

WIZARD

THE GUIDE TO COMICS•68

$4.55 US APRIL 1997 $5.99 CAN.

68a X-MAN (April 1997)
PENCILER: Roger Cruz
INKER: Wellington Diaz
COLORIST: Twilight Graphics

As trendy as a Members Only jacket. While many covers stand the test of time, some—those focusing on a property that was hot for only a short time—make you look back and scratch your head. "X-Man? Who's X-Man?" A spinoff from the monstrously popular "Age of Apocalypse" X-Men crossover, X-Man was such a powerful mutant (which Cruz focused on in his sketches **[top right]**) that his story could only end one of two ways: either he dies from a power overload, or he eventually destroys the Marvel Universe. Several years later, the Marvel Universe is still here.

68b SUPERMAN (April 1997)
PENCILER: Stuart Immonen
INKER: Jose Marzan Jr.
COLORIST: Patrick Martin

The goal was to show as much of Superman's new costume—which was making headlines across the country—as possible, which Immonen's sketches did nicely **[middle and bottom right]**. The final cover design drove the point home by having the "new" Superman holding his old duds.

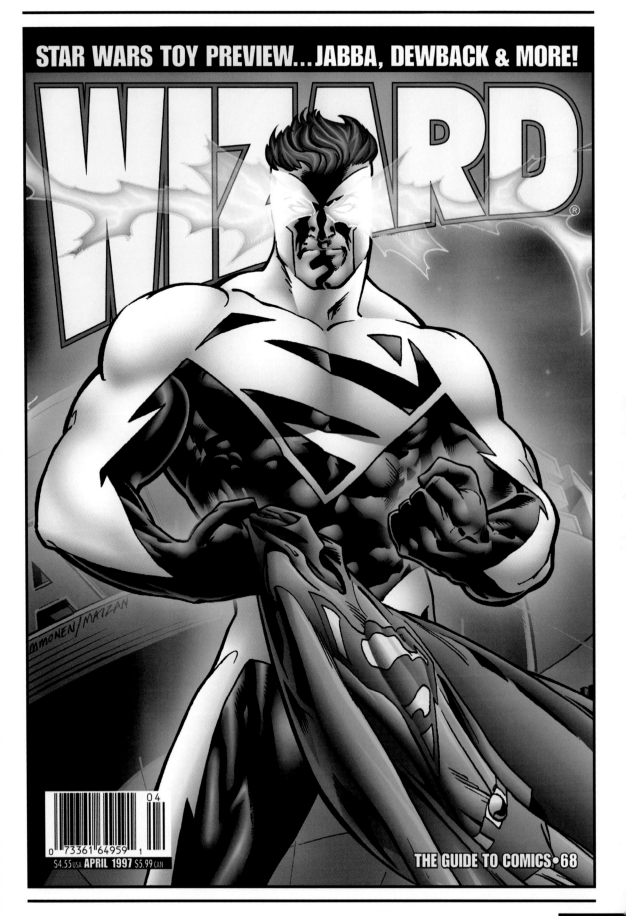

STAR WARS TOY PREVIEW... JABBA, DEWBACK & MORE!

WIZARD

THE GUIDE TO COMICS•68

$4.55 USA **APRIL 1997** $5.99 CAN

0 73361 64959 1

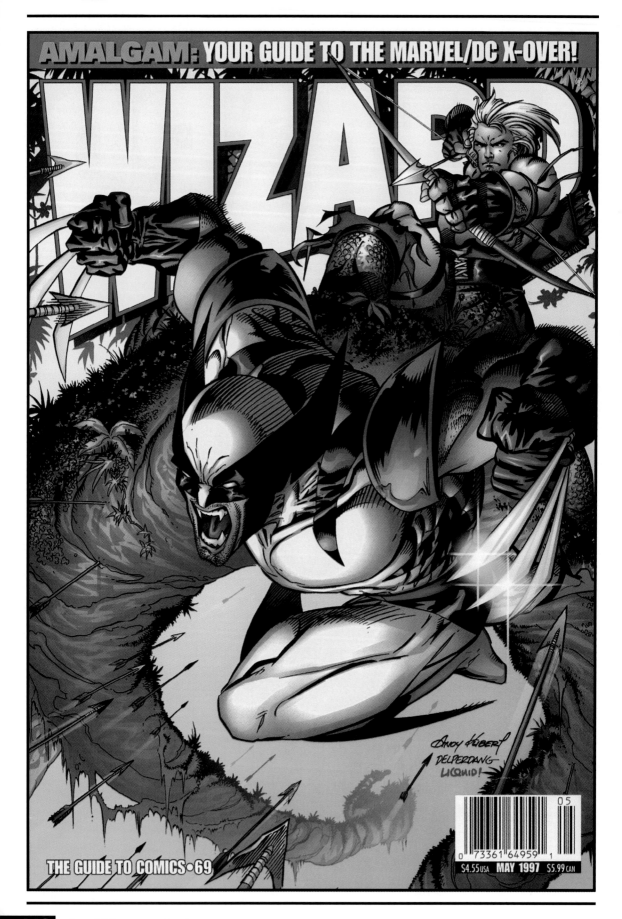

69a

WOLVERINE
(May 1997)
PENCILER: Andy Kubert
INKER: Jesse Delperdang
COLORIST: Liquid Graphics

Originally slated as a solo Ka-Zar cover based off of the character's successful series at the time, it was decided to "play it safe" and add a proven element to the mix: Wolverine. By the time we received Kubert's sketch **[directly below]**, we opted to transform it into a dominant Wolverine cover with Ka-Zar making little more than a cameo appearance. So sad. And no Zabu, either.

AMALGAM: YOUR GUIDE TO THE MARVEL/DC X-OVER!

WIZARD

THE GUIDE TO COMICS • 69

$4.55 USA   MAY 1997 $5.99 CAN

69b

DARK CLAW (May 1997)
PENCILER/INKER: Ty Templeton
COLORIST: Twilight Graphics

We put Dark Claw, a DC/Marvel "Amalgam" character that mixed elements of Batman and Wolverine (previously seen on *Wizard* #56a), on the cover a second time to tie into the second wave of Amalgam Comics. To mix it up a bit, we shunned the more traditional comic book art style, and instead paid homage to the "Batman: The Animated Series" style.

Since our first Darkclaw cover featured a solo shot of the character, we decided with this image to add some baddies. From left: Bloodcrow, Spiral Harley, Hyena and the Two-Faced Goblin.

THE GUIDE TO COMICS •70

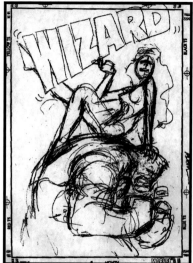

70a GREEN LANTERN (June 1997)
PENCILER: Darryl Banks
INKER: Terry Austin
COLORIST: Twilight Graphics

Not just the first solo Green Lantern cover, but the first time the character appeared on the cover, period. (He almost snuck in on the cover to *Wizard* #57, but got cropped out.)

The initial sketch [top right] featured a much happier, overly-caffeinated GL, but we wanted a grittier, more action-oriented cover.

70b HULK (June 1997)
PENCILER: Adam Kubert
INKER: Mark Farmer
COLORIST: Twilight Graphics

Man…She-Hulk just can't catch a break. This was the fourth time the jade giantess was slated for a *Wizard* cover (issue #14 and two variants on #16), but after multiple sketches featuring her and her more famous cousin were commissioned [middle and bottom right], the decision was made to drop her and focus more on the Hulk. One day we'll get her on the cover—right after that Stingray/Union Jack gatefold.

EXCLUSIVE: THE FUTURE OF MARVEL'S 'HEROES REBORN'

WIZARD

$4.55 USA **JUNE 1997** $5.99 CAN

THE GUIDE TO COMICS 70

0 73361 64959 1

06

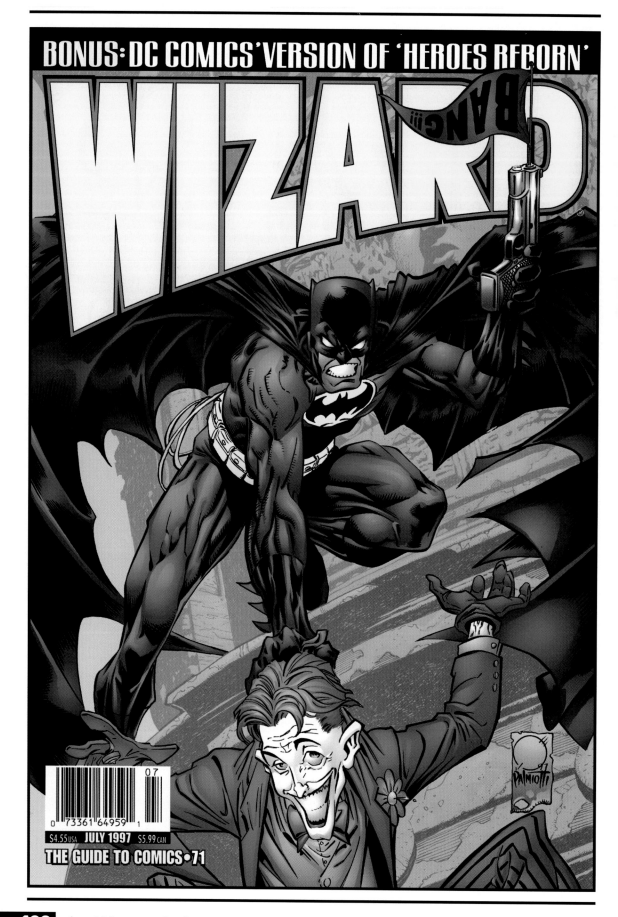

71a

BATMAN (July 1997)
PENCILER: Joe Quesada
INKER: Jimmy Palmiotti
COLORIST: Liquid Graphics

While initially slated as a solo Batman cover **[above]**, we went with a more dynamic concept by adding the Joker to the mix. Batman always presents a design challenge on *Wizard* covers. We strive for bright, colorful images that jump off the page, yet Batman doesn't quite "feel" right when not presented as a shadowy creature of the night.

It's a thin tightrope to walk, and looking back at this cover, we wonder if we did the characters and the intricate background art a disservice by muting the color in favor of starker contrast.

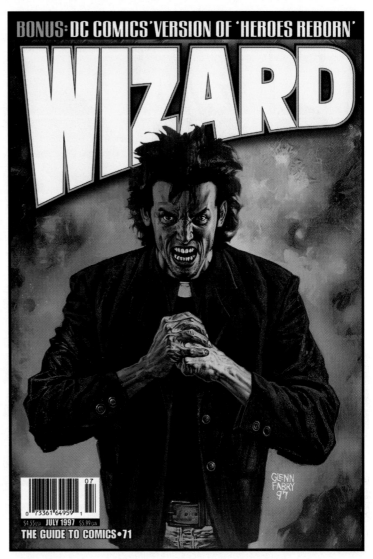

BONUS: DC COMICS' VERSION OF 'HEROES REBORN'

WIZARD

GLENN FABRY 97

$4.55 USA   JULY 1997 $5.99 CAN
THE GUIDE TO COMICS • 71

07
0 73361 64959 1

71b

PREACHER (July 1997)
PAINTER: Glenn Fabry

A red-hot DC/Vertigo series at the time, a *Preacher*-based cover was a no-brainer for us. But to insure the image—based on a mature-readers title—would be acceptable to the various outlets where *Wizard* is sold, we decided to avoid putting cigarettes on the cover. Or booze. Or guns. Or anything even remotely *Preacher*-like. We can be so lame sometimes.

After playing with the idea of going for a full-cast shot with Cassidy, Tulip and Jesse **[right]**, we went with a more dominant shot of Jesse, the series' star.

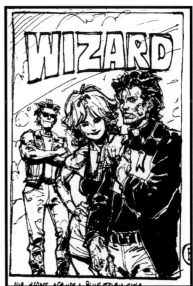

72a
X-MEN
(August 1997)
PENCILER: Joe Madureira

INKER: Tim Townsend
COLORIST: Liquid Graphics

No, really…these two were X-Men. The initial sketch **[below]** had more of a focus on Dr. Cecilia Reyes, but we felt the hulking Maggot character looked more dynamic, and we asked Madureira to rework the image.

Arms overhead - Towering pose
Her running in from the side.

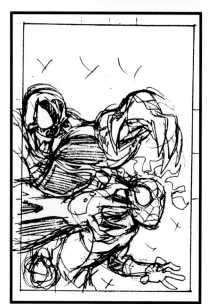

72b
SPIDER-MAN (August 1997)
PENCILER/INKER: Mike Wieringo
COLORIST: Twilight Graphics

One of our favorite Spider-Man covers, because it was laid out so well and we dig the characters. Spider-Man—the most important cover element—crouches front and center, well-lit and easily recognizable; Venom frames him perfectly; they're in dynamic poses; there's in-your-face action…artist Mike Wieringo just nailed a really cool cover. A thin white outline was added around Venom's body to help him pop off that dark background.

The initial cover sketch **[at left]** saw Venom giving Spidey a wet willie.

BONUS: GEN13'S NEW MEMBERS, WHO'S IN & WHO'S OUT!
WIZARD®
08
0 73361 64959 1
$4.55USA AUGUST 1997 $5.99CAN
THE GUIDE TO COMICS•72

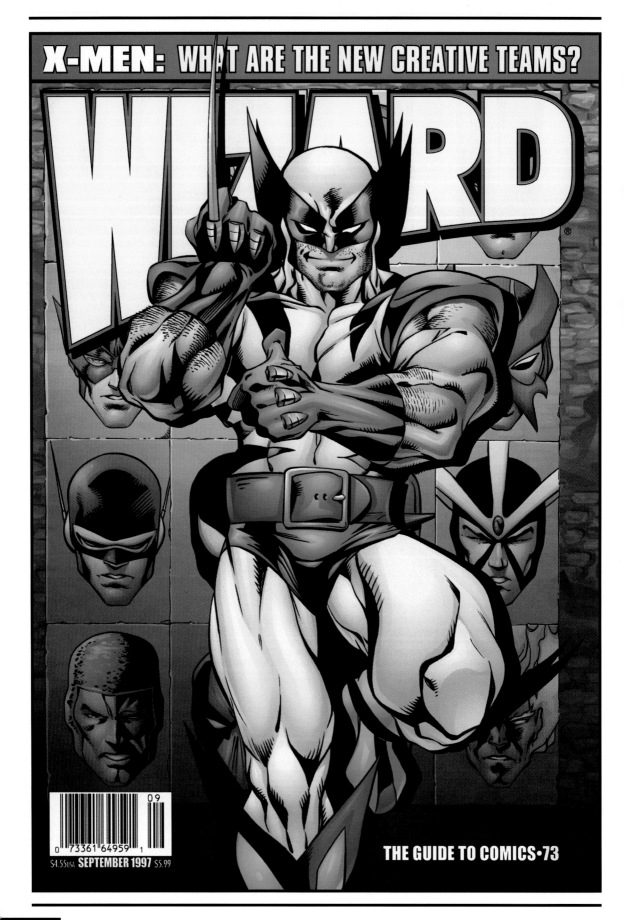

73a WOLVERINE

(September 1997)
PENCILER: Carlos Pacheco
INKER: Jimmy Palmiotti
COLORIST: Liquid Graphics

We tied this cover to an interior feature counting down the best superhero costumes ever designed. The *Wizard* staff indulged themselves by putting headshots of their favorite "non-A-list" characters as part of the background montage.

The background montage **[above]** featured, from left: Black Panther, Yellowjacket I, Stealth Armor Iron Man, Nova I, Iron Man, Hawkeye, Spider-Man, Jack of Hearts, Spider-Man (black suit), Sunfire, Vision, Prowler, Firelord, Captain America, Havok and Daredevil.

X-MEN: WHAT ARE THE NEW CREATIVE TEAMS?

Sin City

WIZARD

THE GUIDE TO COMICS • 73

SEPTEMBER 1997 $4.99

0 73361 64959 1 09

73b SIN CITY'S MIHO

(September 1997)
PENCILER/INKER: Frank Miller
COLORIST: Twilight Graphics

A last minute call from Dark Horse pushing for a Frank Miller *Sin City* cover bumped back the Nightwing cover we had planned for this issue (which ended up running in #74, see next page). Similar to the previous Sin City cover, it would break *Wizard* tradition and not run full-color.

Note the gatefold JLA cover by Howard Porter and Jimmy Palmiotti **[at left]** that had been created for *Wizard*, but by this point we had shied away from running fold-out covers. Luckily we found a home for it as a poster insert in our first *JLA Special* published a few months later.

74a

NIGHTWING
(October 1997)
PENCILER: Scott McDaniel

INKER: Karl Story

COLORIST: Twilight Graphics

Originally slated for #73, this would be the first time Nightwing appeared on a *Wizard* cover. While both the initial cover sketch **[directly below]** and final cover featured a dynamic action pose, we went with the version that focused more on Nigtwing's face.

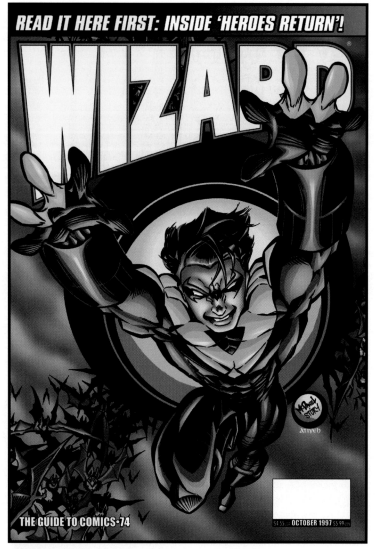

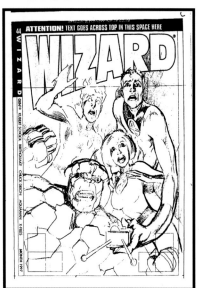

74b

THE FANTASTIC FOUR (October 1997)
PENCILER: Alan Davis

INKER: Mark Farmer

COLORIST: Liquid Graphics

We tied this cover into Marvel Entertainment's massive "Heroes Return" event, which saw its principal characters—Iron Man, Captain America, the core Avengers and Fantastic Four—return to the "regular" Marvel Universe after a year-long absence. It would be only the second time the entire team—clockwise from top left: the Thing, Mr. Fantastic, Invisible Woman and the Human Torch—had scored its own *Wizard* cover (*Wizard* #55, though individual members share covers with other characters on issues #42 and #67).

Note that one of Alan Davis' original sketches **[bottom left]** featured the team screening the unreleased "Fantastic Four" film by Roger Corman.

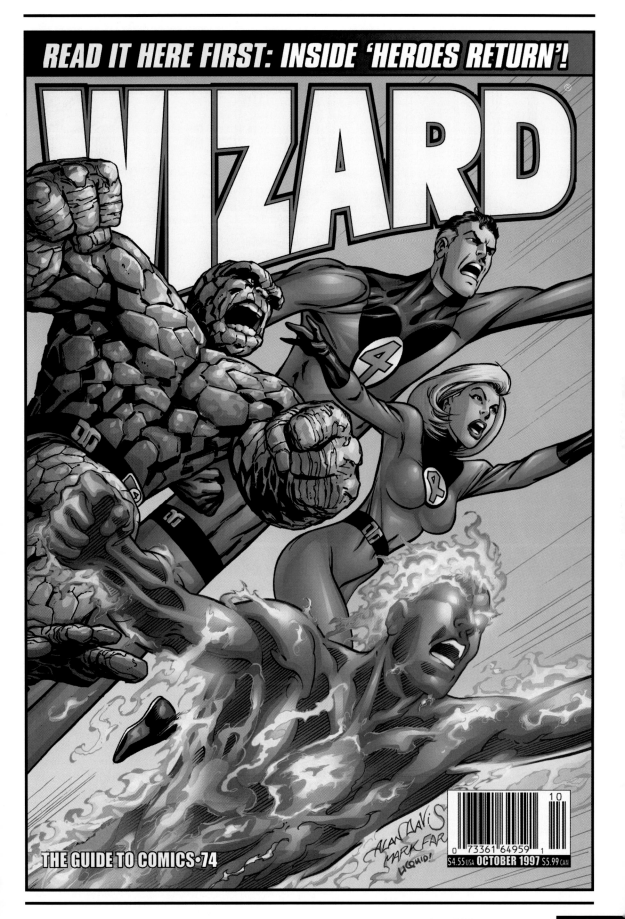

READ IT HERE FIRST: INSIDE 'HEROES RETURN'!

WIZARD

THE GUIDE TO COMICS·74

$4.55 USA **OCTOBER 1997** $5.99 CAN

0 73361 64959 1

WOLVERINE #1/2 EXCLUSIVE COMIC OFFER!

WIZARD

THE GUIDE TO COMICS • 75

$4.55 USA NOVEMBER 1997 $5.99 CAN

0 73361 64959 1

75a

JLA
(November 1997)
PAINTER: Alex Ross

Designed as a two-panel cover **[at right]**, the piece was trimmed down due to our move away from gatefolds. Why the move to single panels? Advertisers were going through a phase where they wouldn't buy expensive gatefold ads to place behind our expensive gatefold covers. Fortunately, Alex Ross understood and we ran the full image as a poster placed inside issue #75's polybag. Later the Warner Bros. Studio Store produced a lithograph the same size as the original painting.

Clockwise from bottom left: Wonder Woman (with the Atom on her shoulder), Batman, Superman, Martian Manhunter, Hawkgirl, Hawkman, Flash, Red Tornado, Zatanna, Aquaman, Green Lantern, Enlongated Man, Green Arrow and Black Canary (with mascot Snapper Carr's hand at the bottom right).

75b

LADY DEATH
(November 1997)
PENCILER/INKER: Steven Hughes
COLORIST: Twilight Graphics

First Lady Death cover. Both the initial sketch **[above]** and the final cover had a strong Halloween theme, but we felt the classic "riding the broomstick" worked better. Don't read into it.

76a

DARKNESS
(December 1997)
PENCILER: Marc Silvestri

INKER: Batt
COLORIST: Steve Firchow

The planned Wolverine/Rogue cover by Kevin Lau **[directly below]** was bumped in favor of the Darkness, tying into Top Cow's then-latest launch by superstar artist Marc Silvestri. The Wolverine/Rogue cover would never run or progress past this initial sketch form.

This issue marks an official tagline change from the more vague *Guide to Comics* to a more concise *The Comics Magazine*. With our circulation quickly expanding into mainstream venues, we felt the title needed to clearly communicate what *Wizard* is all about to casual consumers.

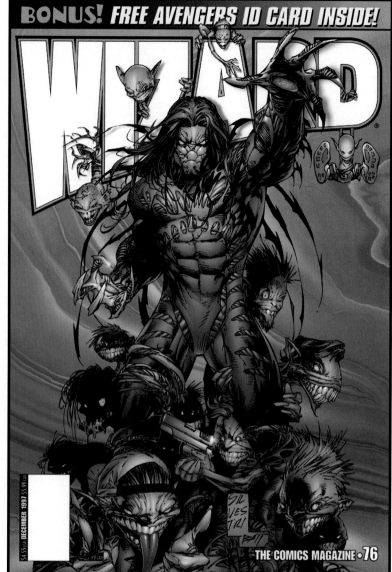

76b

CAPTAIN AMERICA
(December 1997)
PENCILER: George Pérez

INKER: Jimmy Palmiotti
COLORIST: Liquid Graphics

Hard to believe, but this—the 76th issue of *Wizard*—featured our first George Pérez illustrated cover. We tapped the legendary artist to tackle the iconic Captain America besting his longtime nemesis the Red Skull. Pérez's other two sketches testify to his immense talent **[both at left]**—both presented dynamic cover possibilities, and we couldn't have gone wrong running any of them. To sum up: Pérez is the goods.

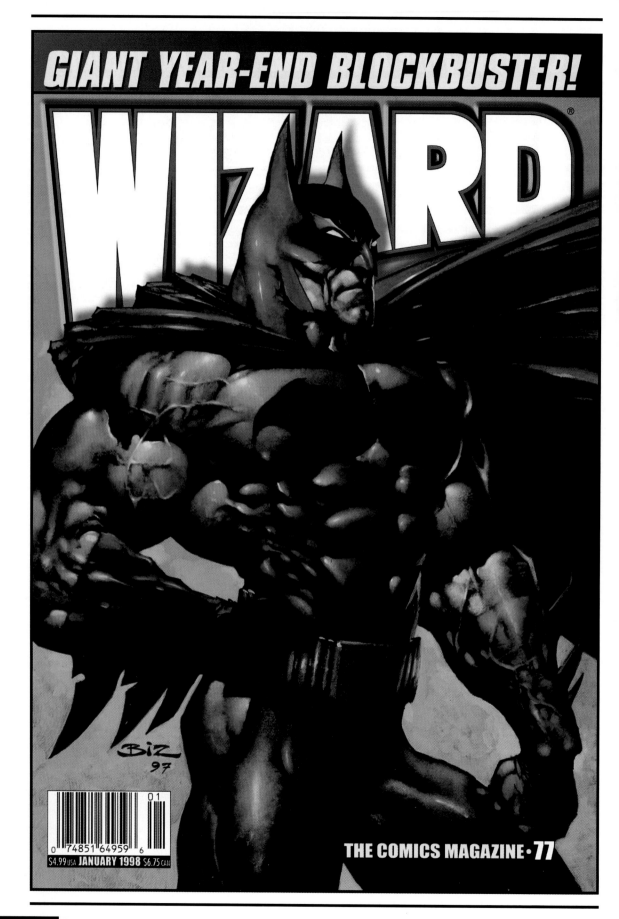

77a

BATMAN (January 1998)
PENCILER: Simon Bisley
Wanting to do something different for the '98 Year-End issue, we went with the theme of famous painters doing top tier characters. We tapped Simon Bisley for Batman and fantasy painter Fred Fields for Spawn.

77b

SPAWN (January 1998)
PAINTER: Fred Fields
Field's initial sketches for the cover **[middle and bottom right]** featured close-up shots of Spawn, but we wanted a more full-figure pose to compliment the Bisley Batman cover variant.

We had assigned Ed McGuinness to draw us up a Deadpool cover **[top right]**, but after months of postponing it, the image would never see print as a cover. It would eventually run as a poster insert in *Wizard*'s 1999 *PosterMania* magazine.

78a

CLIFFHANGER
(February 1998)
PENCILERS: Joe Madureira, J. Scott Campbell and Humberto Ramos
INKER: Alex Garner
COLORISTS: Liquid Graphics and Wildstorm

After we announced that artists Joe Madureira, J. Scott Campbell and Humberto Ramos would launch their own imprint called Cliffhanger, we had the creators put together a jam cover featuring (from top) Garrison from Madureira's *Battle Chasers*, Alex Elder from Ramos' *Crimson* and Abbey Chase from Campbell's *Danger Girl*. This would be Ramos' first *Wizard* cover.

78b

SPIDER-MAN
(February 1998)
PENCILER/INKER: Steve Skroce
COLORIST: Liquid Graphics

We wanted a simple, clean Spidey cover...no exploding pumpkins, no alien parasites, no fat guys with big metal arms. The initial sketches looked moody **[far left]** and exciting **[immediate left]**, but not as dynamic as the final cover.

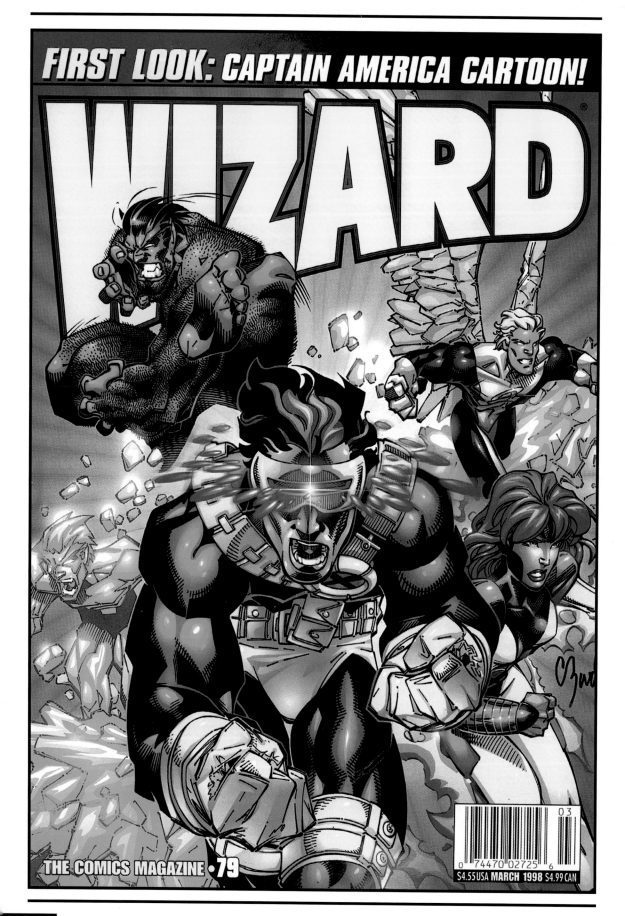

79a

X-MEN (March 1998)
PENCILER: Chris Bachalo
INKER: Tim Townsend
COLORIST: Liquid Graphics

After several sketches trying to incorporate more of the X-Men's sizeable roster **[below]**, we took the cover down a different route. Here the original 1963 X-Men roster (clockwise from top left: Beast, Archangel, Jean Grey, Cyclops and Iceman) as they appeared in 1998. Most have turned blue.

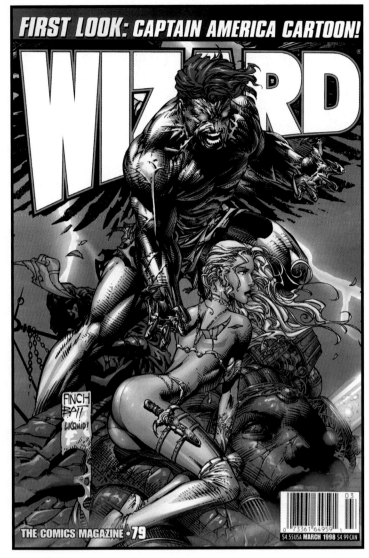

79b

ASCENSION (March 1998)
PENCILER: David Finch
INKER: Batt
COLORIST: Liquid Graphics

When the final art arrived for the cover, our sales department did a double-take. Turns out the young lady (Andromeda, crouching next to Lucien) wore a thong so thin you could floss with it (the topic of most German websites). We asked the colorist to extend the thong into more of a bikini bottom in an effort to prevent problems with the more conservative retail outlets that carry *Wizard*.

80a

SOUTH PARK
(April 1998)
ART: courtesy of Comedy Central

First South Park cover. The animated show's popularity was staggering and fit the tone of *Wizard* perfectly. We're still doing our best to convince the Sales Department to greenlight a Timmy cover. "TIMAY!"

80b

WOLVERINE VS. HULK (April 1998)
PENCILER/INKER: Leinil Francis Yu
COLORIST: Liquid Graphics

The initial sketch **[left]** featured the Hulk in a more prominent position, but we had the cover reworked to showcase Wolverine more strongly.

80c

THOR (April 1998)
PENCILER: John Romita Jr.
INKER: Mark Farmer
COLORIST: Liquid Graphics

Pushing for a Thor solo cover since issue #7 (which almost happened with Walt Simonson attached, but never worked out), we were finally given the okay to pursue the image since it tied into Marvel's relaunch of the character. Here the Norse God of Thunder smites evil-doers amidst a giant bowl of pasta.

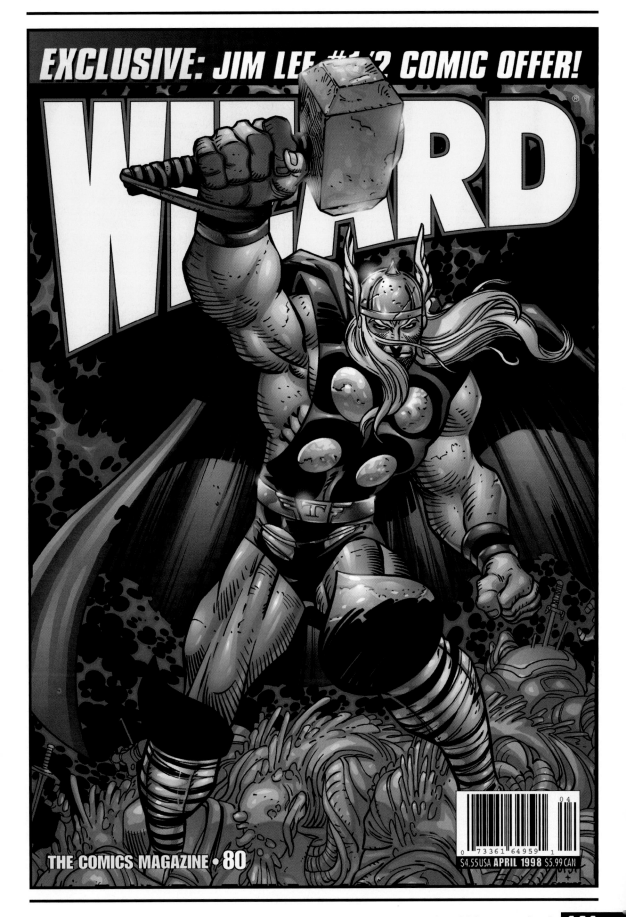

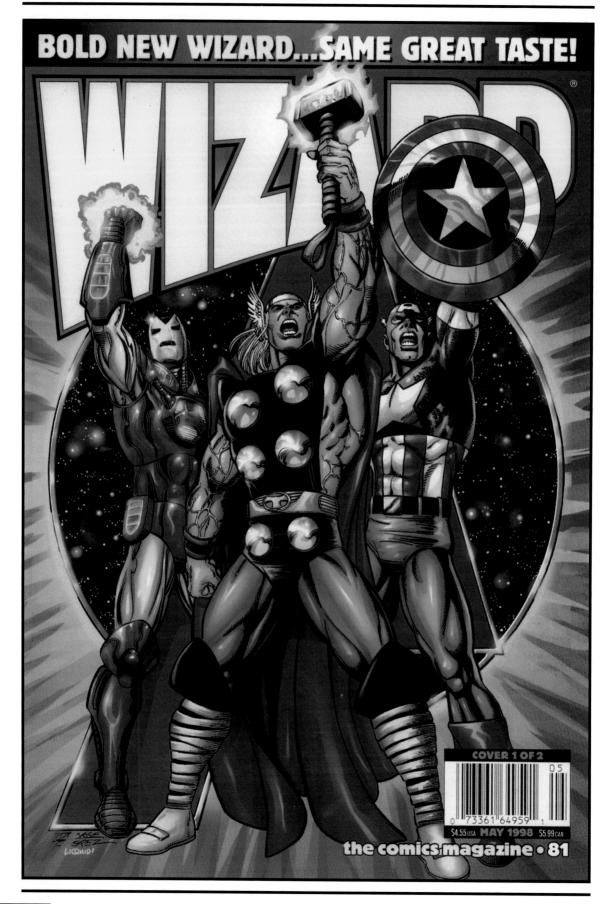

81a

AVENGERS (May 1998)
PENCILER/INKER: George Pérez
COLORIST: Liquid Graphics

We celebrated the debut of *Wizard*'s redesign (i.e., new departments, new looks, etc.) with a Pérez-drawn Avengers cover (from left: Iron Man, Thor and Captain America) tying into the red-hot relaunch of the series. We had played with a dozen variants of the background color and it came down to purple or green **[left]**. One noteworthy coloring gaff: we overlooked that the middle stripe on Cap's belly should be red, not white. We dropped and gave him 20.

81b

CABLE (May 1998)
PENCILER/INKER: Ladrónn
COLORIST: Liquid Graphics

While the first sketch **[bottom left]** had too much background and not enough Cable for a *Wizard* cover, the second sketch **[middle left]** makes us wonder why we didn't go with the more dynamic action shot, which would only have to be slightly tweaked as to not cover so much of the *Wizard* logo.

82a

JLA (June 1998)
PENCILER: Howard Porter
INKER: John Dell
COLORIST: Liquid Graphics

Originally slated as a JLA: The Nail
cover by Alan Davis and Mark
Farmer (featuring an Elseworlds
JLA with an Amish Superman), that
cover [below] was reworked to a
more mainstream JLA image
featuring Batman, Superman &
Wonder Woman.

82b

IRON MAN
(June 1998)
PENCILER: Sean Chen
INKER: Eric J. Cannon
COLORIST: Liquid Graphics

Can Iron Man save Luke, Leia and Han
from the trash compactor?!?
We wanted an Iron Man cover (the
character's first solo appearance and
a nod to his relaunched ongoing
series), but we also wanted something different in the presentation.
Artist Sean Chen hit the nail on the
head with his claustrophobic images
[sketches at left]. Chen even put the
cherry on top by suggesting and
drawing a "crushed" logo for further
effect.

83a

SUPER-BABES
(July 1998)
PENCILER/INKER/COLORIST:
Adam Hughes

Receiving word from the marketing department that this would be the final gatefold cover to run on *Wizard* for the foreseeable future, we sent it off with a bang. On this variant cover we tapped artist Adam Hughes to do what he does better than anyone in the business: sultry women. But not just any women. This cover would shine the spotlight on the industry's highest profile female superheroes. From left: Witchblade, Supergirl, Rogue, Wonder Woman, Fairchild, Invisible Woman, Catwoman and Scarlet Witch.

The initial sketch **[above]** featured six characters, but we asked Hughes to add Catwoman and the Scarlet Witch to the final version.

She-Hulk was initially considered to appear on the cover, but was dropped in favor of the equally-hulking Fairchild character, making this the fifth time the jade giantess—who has never appeared on a *Wizard* cover—almost appeared on the cover.

Cue heartfelt Kermit melody.

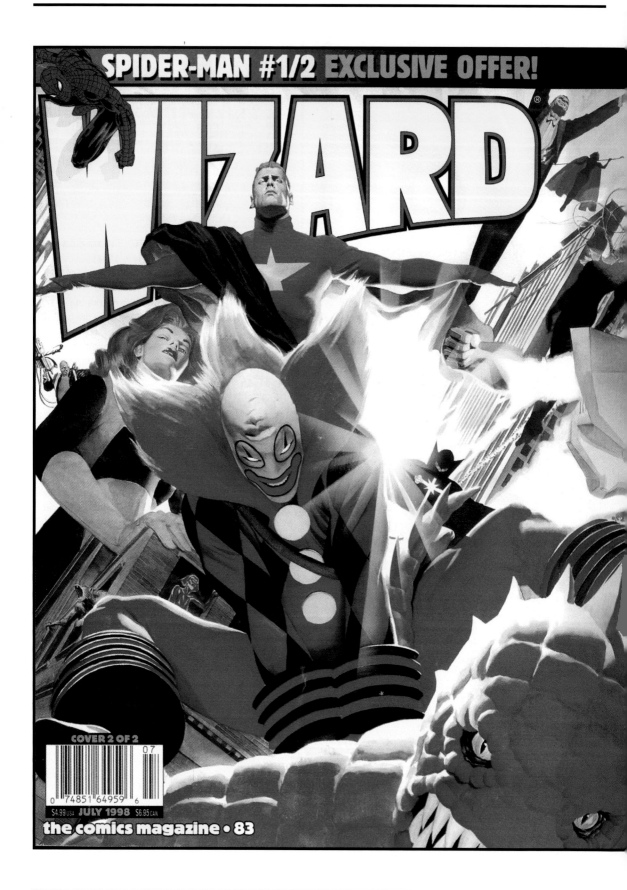

83b

ASTRO CITY
(July 1998)
PAINTER: Alex Ross

So what could hold its own opposite an Adam Hughes über-babes cover (see previous page)? Two words: Alex Ross. Here, the superstar artist closed out the *Wizard* gatefold era with style, bringing the heroes of Astro City to life in a manner no one else on the planet could possibly emulate. The last gatefold *Wizard* cover—which set a record for characters on a cover with 33—featured, in no particular order, The First Family: Augustus First, Julius First, Nick First, Rex, Natalie and Astra; The Honor Guard: Samaritan, Beautie, Black Rapier, Cleopatra, M.P.H., N-Forcer, Quarrel and Max O'-Millions; The Astro City Irregulars: Ruby, Robo, Roach, Jailbait, Juice and Stray; The Crossbreed: Noah, David, Daniel, Joshua, Mary and Peter; Jack-in-the-Box; Confessor; Hanged Man; Crackerjack; Nightingale; Sunbird and Winged Victory.

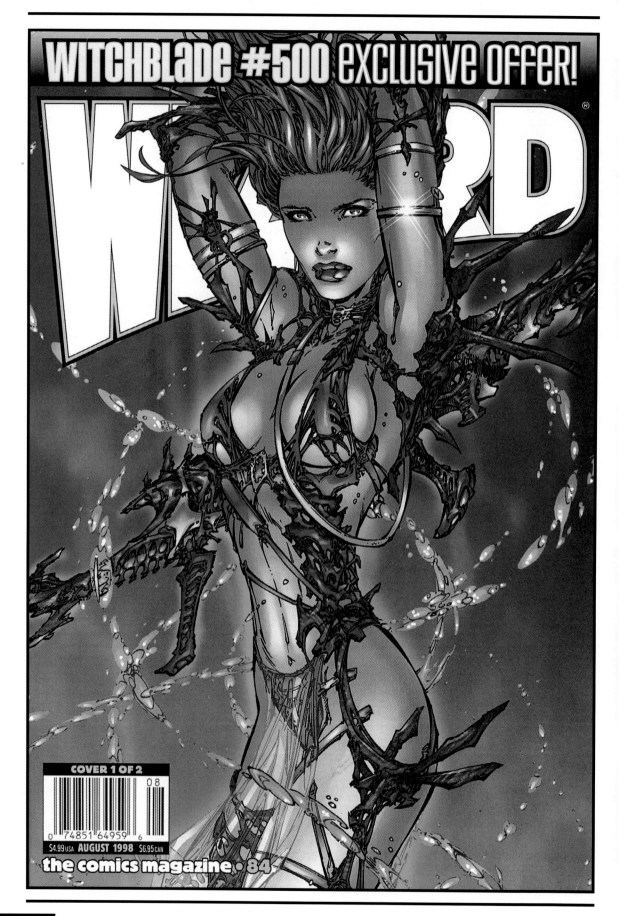

84a FATHOM (August 1998)

PENCILER: Michael Turner

INKER: Joe Weems

COLORIST: J.D. Smith

First Fathom cover. We went with more of a glamour shot than an action pose.

84b SPIDER-MAN (August 1998)

PENCILER/INKER: Mike Wieringo

COLORIST: Liquid Graphics

Borrowing the concept from an earlier *Wizard* cover (#73a), here Spider-Man clings to a billboard featuring the multiple costumes he's appeared in. The first sketch **[below left]** had Spidey looking at the billboard, which didn't work for us (most successful cover subjects stare out towards the consumer). The second sketch **[below middle]** was closer to what we were looking for. The background sketch **[below right]** showcases all of Spidey's various incarnations. From top left: Spider-Armor, Cosmic Spider-Man, Hornet, Kaine, Ricochet, Spidey in black costume, Peter Parker, Scarlet Spider, Dusk, Ben Reilly, Spider-Man 2099, Spidey w/ paper bag over his head, Peter as masked wrestler, Spider-Man, Spider-Kid and Prodigy.

The *Wizard* staff added Peter Porker, the Spectacular Spider-Ham in the final art (see final cover, lower right). Peter Porker: 1, She-Hulk: 0.

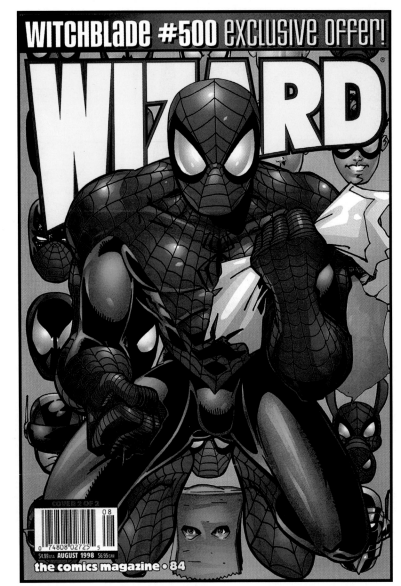

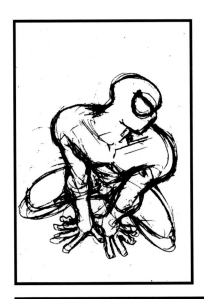

85a SUPERMAN
(September 1998)
PENCILER/INKER: Tim Sale

COLORIST: Bjärne Hansen

Originally created as an image for our discontinued poster insert program to tie into the release of *Superman For All Seasons*, this piece of art found a home as a cover even though it didn't quite fit our cover measurements. The result was a great piece of art awkwardly fitted for a cover.

85b AVENGERS (September 1998)
PENCILER/INKER: Rick Burchett
COLORIST: Brimstone

Our goal was to create buzz with this cover image. See, there wasn't an Avengers cartoon at the time, so we aped the "Batman: The Animated Series" art style and presented the Avengers (clockwise from top: Iron Man, Thor, Hawkeye, Captain America, Scarlet Witch and the Vision) in that fashion. The result? Some annoyed fans. They felt the cover mislead them with a project that didn't exist. Our lesson learned, we'd handle gimmick covers like this much more carefully in the future.

In hindsight, Rick Burchett's original sketch **[at left]** had a cooler pose for Cap, but the final layout for the rest of the team really worked out well.

85c WOLVERINE AND SUPERMAN (September 1998)
PENCILER: Kevin Maguire
INKER: Al Gordon

COLORIST: Liquid Graphics

One of the more challenging *Wizard* covers ever created. For a behind the scenes look at the steps involved in the creation of a *Wizard* cover (using this one as the example), check out page 188.

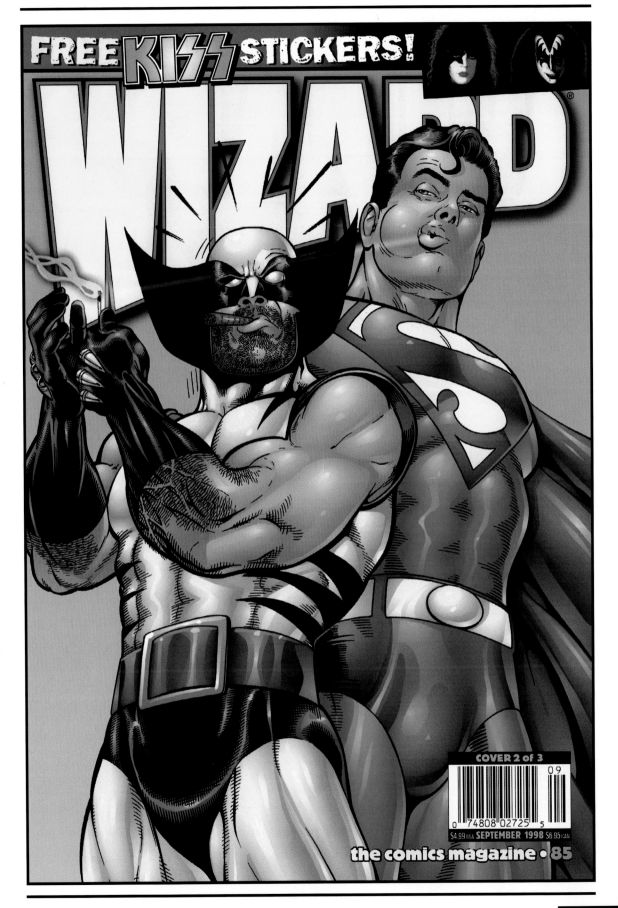

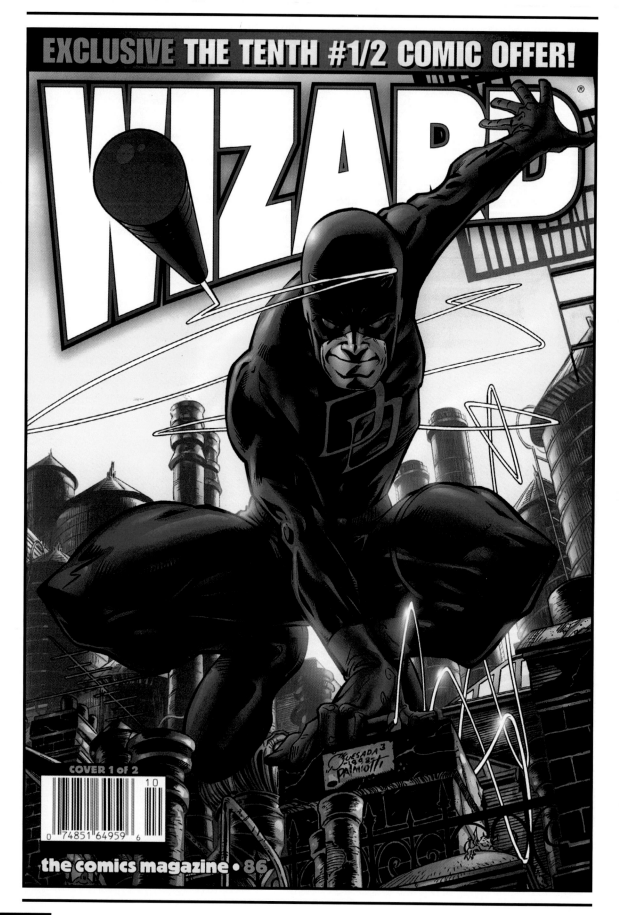

86a

DAREDEVIL (October 1998)
PENCILER: Joe Quesada
INKER: Jimmy Palmiotti
COLORIST: Brian Haberlin

Many consider this to be one of the most definitive Daredevil illustrations ever created. If nothing else, it's one of *Wizard*'s most dynamic covers. Aside from being a scary-talented artist, Joe Quesada has a unique understanding of how a cover illustration is composed differently than a pin up, poster or interior comic page. Besides channeling energy through DD's comin-atcha pose, Quesada amps things up by tilting the camera angle, as well as creating a 3-D-like illusion of depth with the rapidly uncoiling billy club.

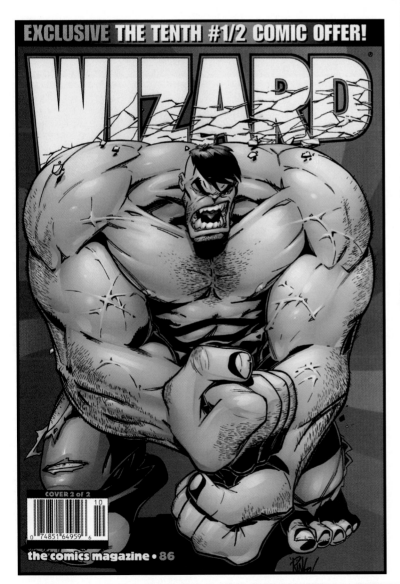

86b

HULK
(October 1998)
PENCILER/INKER: Mike Wieringo
COLORIST: Liquid Graphics

We approached artist Mike Wieringo with a single goal for this Hulk image: Make it so the jade giant didn't quite fit on the cover. The first two sketches fit the bill **[above]**, but would have obscured too much of the *Wizard* logo. The final version saw the poor logo feeling the impact of Hulk's mass.

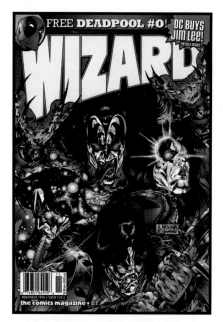

87a
KISS (November 1998)
PENCILER: Angel Medina
INKER: Kevin Conrad
COLORIST: Brian Haberlin

Four characters on a cover pose a challenge to the artist because they can clutter it up. We turned to artist Joe Quesada to help compose this cover image, and he found a way to make it work with the four members of KISS (clockwise from top: KISS members the Demon, Starchild, the Cat and Space Ace). Because of his superior design skills, we would ask Quesada to lay out over a dozen *Wizard* covers that he himself didn't have time to pencil.

87b
PUNISHER (November 1998)
PENCILER: Joe Quesada
INKER: Jimmy Palmiotti
COLORIST: Brian Haberlin

The first time Punisher ever appeared on a *Wizard* cover. Ironically enough, it was in his least successful incarnation, the short-lived "demon-hunter Punisher."

87c
DARK KNIGHTS (November 1998)
PENCILER/INKER: Mark Texeira
COLORIST: Liquid Graphics

This Halloween-themed "heroes of the night" cover features (from top) Spawn, Batman and Ghost Rider. We went with a layout of the three standing close to each other, rather than having them scattered **[left]**. This would also be the first time Ghost Rider made a cover without the trademark pointy *Wizard* cap design element from our early days (issues #2 and #13). You're welcome, Johnny Blaze.

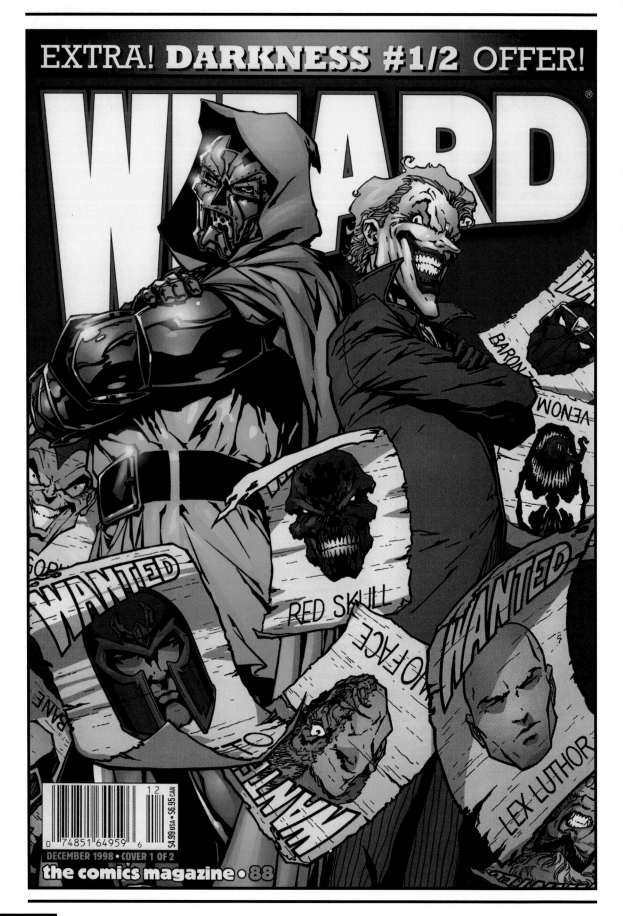

88a

JOKER AND DOOM
(December 1998)
PENCILER/INKER: Jim Calafiore
COLORIST: Liquid Graphics

Another villains-only theme cover, here we teamed the greatest villains from the Marvel and DC universes. The initial design had the pair against a wall plastered with wanted posters of other villains **[directly below]**, but we felt the "swirling leaflets" approach appeared more dynamic. Nice touch on artist Jim Calafiore's part with the "Wanted" logos drawn in the same style as the *Wizard* logo.

88b

BATTLE CHASERS **(December 1998)**
PENCILER: Joe Madureira
INKER: Tim McWeeney
COLORIST: Liquid Graphics

Another example of hindsight always being 20/20. As cool as the final cover is (featuring Gully and Callibreto), the unused sketch **[bottom left]** would have made for a unique cover. Ah well. Maybe it ran on the Earth 2 *Wizard*.

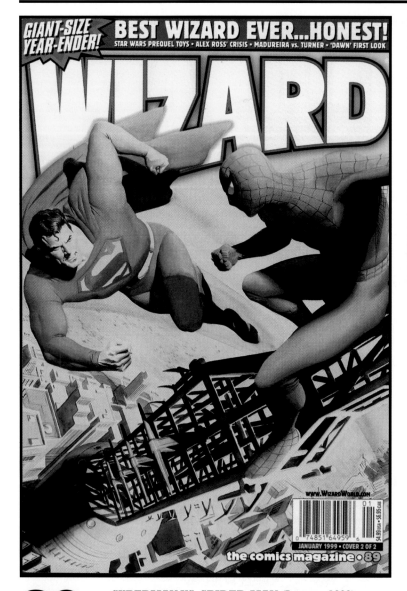

89a SUPERMAN VS. SPIDER-MAN (January 1999)
PAINTER: Alex Ross

Wanting a cross-company cover to celebrate this Year-End edition of *Wizard*, we penciled in a Superman/Spider-Man image. We contacted artist Alex Ross to see if he was interested, and he said yes, but only if he could use the opportunity to pay homage to the 1976 *Superman vs. Spider-Man* oversized comic cover illustrated by Ross Andru **[top right]**.

89b BATMAN (January 1999)
PENCILER: Jim Lee
INKER: Scott Williams
COLORIST: Tad Ehrlich

Years before he would become the regular penciler on *Batman* and make it the No. 1 selling comic in North America, Jim Lee whipped up a Dark Knight Detective cover for us. It's actually Lee's second-ever Batman cover, the first being the one that graced *Batman: Black and White* #1 in 1996. The initial sketches **[middle and bottom right]** featured some hard-hitting dialogue.

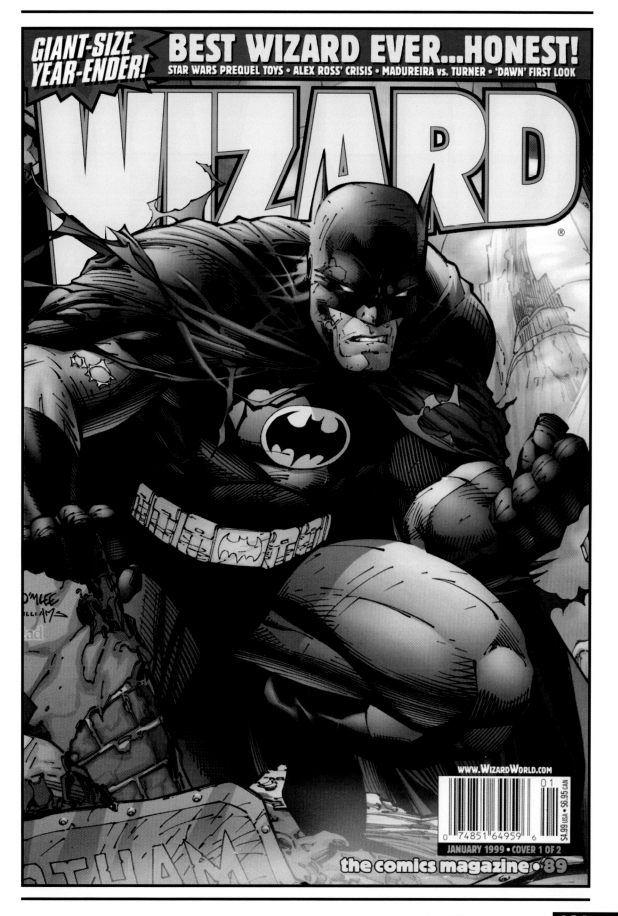

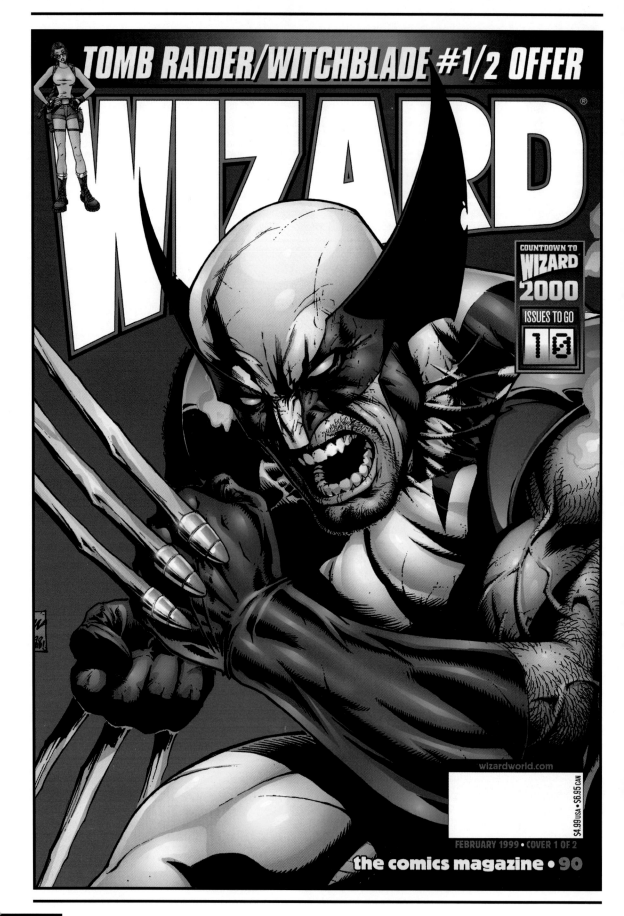

TOMB RAIDER/WITCHBLADE #1/2 OFFER

WIZARD

COUNTDOWN TO
WIZARD
2000
ISSUES TO GO
10

wizardworld.com

$4.99USA • $6.95 CAN

FEBRUARY 1999 • COVER 1 OF 2

the comics magazine • 90

90a
WOLVERINE
(February 1999)
PENCILER/INKER:
Leinil Francis Yu
COLORIST: Liquid Graphics

We began the promotion for *Wizard* #2000—the issue that would ship with the end of the millennium—with a countdown clock clicking down from 10, with each subsequent issue ticking closer to the celebratory issue.

The initial sketch for the cover featured an unmasked Wolverine **[directly below]**, but we felt the cover would be more successful with the recognizable masked version. The second sketch **[bottom]** was closer to what we were looking for.

90b
WITCHBLADE/ TOMB RAIDER
(February 1999)
PENCILER: Michael Turner
INKER: Joe Weems
COLORIST: Jonathan D. Smith

First Tomb Raider cover. The initial sketch **[at right]** looked cool, but we liked the close-up shot of Top Cow's lethal ladies.

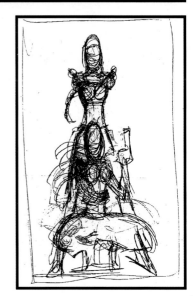

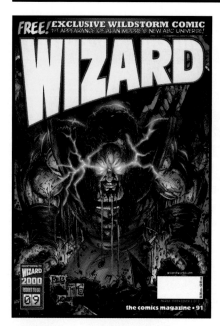

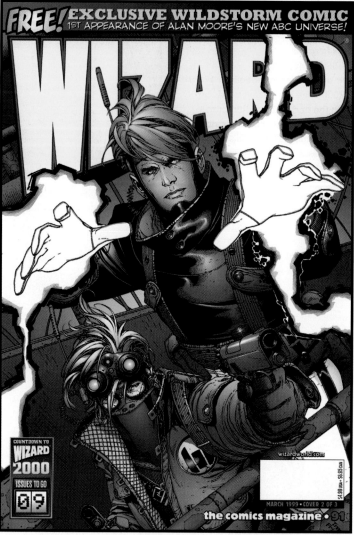

91a

UNDERTAKER
(March 1999)
PENCILER: Rob Brown
INKER: Danny Miki
COLORIST: Liquid Graphics

Normally we strive for lighter, more colorful covers, but this image—featuring WWE superstar wrestler the Undertaker—was a dark, gothic character and the star of his own dark, gothic comic series by dark, gothic publisher Chaos Comics.
The result? An unusually dark, gothic *Wizard* cover.

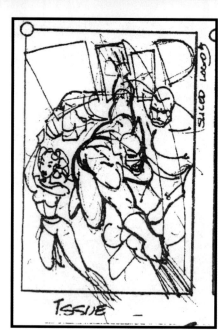

91b

WILDCATS (March 1999)
PENCILER: Travis Charest
INKER: Richard Friend
COLORIST: Wildstorm

The Wildcats characters (here, Spartan and Grifter) return to our cover after a four-year absence. And yes, the "cats" is now lowercase.

91c

X-MEN (March 1999)
PENCILER: J. Scott Campbell
INKER: Alex Garner
COLORIST: Liquid Graphics

The original sketch [at right] featured Wolverine slicing the *Wizard* logo into bite-sized chunks while Shadowcat and Colossus brought up the rear. We had the image reworked to include fan-favorite Nightcrawler for the final piece.

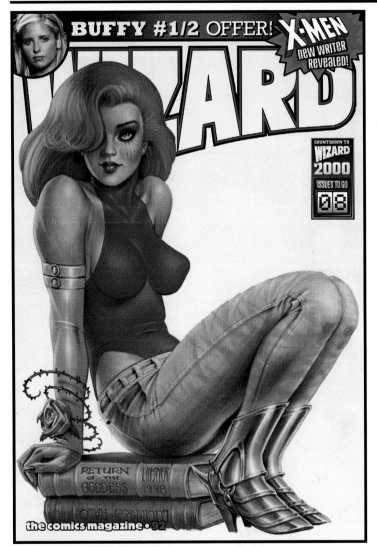

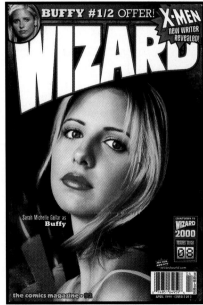

92c **BUFFY** (April 1999)
PHOTO: Courtesy of the WB
This shot of Sarah
Michelle Gellar (from the popular "Buffy:
The Vampire Slayer" TV show) would be
Wizard's first photo cover. We'd experi-
ment a few times with mainstream
images like this, eventually learning that
a more successful photo-cover program
would be those directly tied to comic
book properties, such as the Spider-Man,
X-Men and Hulk movies.

92a **SUPERMAN VS. SPIDER-MAN** (April 1999)
PENCILER: Kevin Maguire
INKER: Al Gordon
COLORIST: Liquid Graphics
We tied this cover into a "Which is better: DC or Marvel?" feature inside
the issue. After a round of sketches by Kevin Maguire didn't quite capture
the feel we were looking for **[at right]**, we turned to artist Joe Quesada to
design the layout that Maguire followed for the final pencils.

92b **DAWN** (April 1999)
PAINTER: Joseph Michael Linsner
While artist Joseph Michael Linsner had drawn a
previous cover (#64a), this would be the first time his most famous
creation—Dawn—would grace a *Wizard* cover.

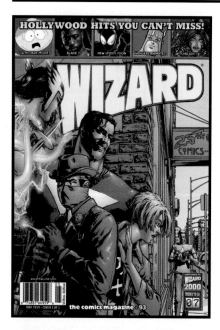

93a

ABC (May 1999)
PENCILER/INKER: Gene Ha
COLORIST: Liquid Graphics

A last-minute cover added to the #93 mix to tie into the launch of DC's America's Best Comics imprint, featuring (clockwise from top left) Promethea, Tom Strong, Toybox and Greyshirt.

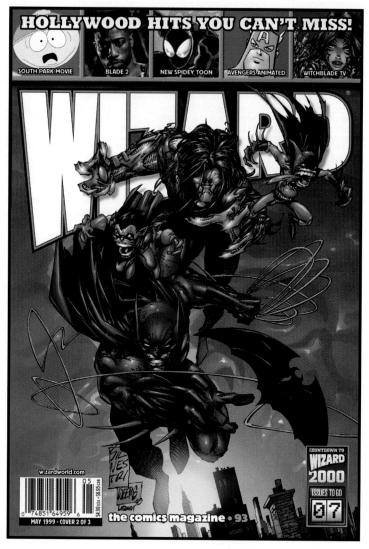

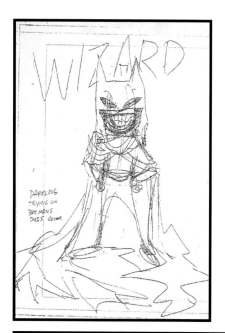

93b

BATMAN/DARKNESS (May 1999)
PENCILER: Marc Silvestri
INKER: Joe Weems

COLORIST: Liquid Graphics

Tying into the DC/Top Cow crossover that saw Batman teaming with the Darkness, Marc Silvestri's original sketch for the cover took a lighthearted approach to the event **[at left]**.

93c

JLA (May 1999)
PENCILER: Joe Madureira
INKER: Tom McWeeney

COLORIST: Liquid Graphics

An example of *Wizard*'s desire to feature dominant images on our covers. While the JLA are a hot property, we boiled down the seven-member team to the top three highest profile members: Superman, Batman and Wonder Woman.

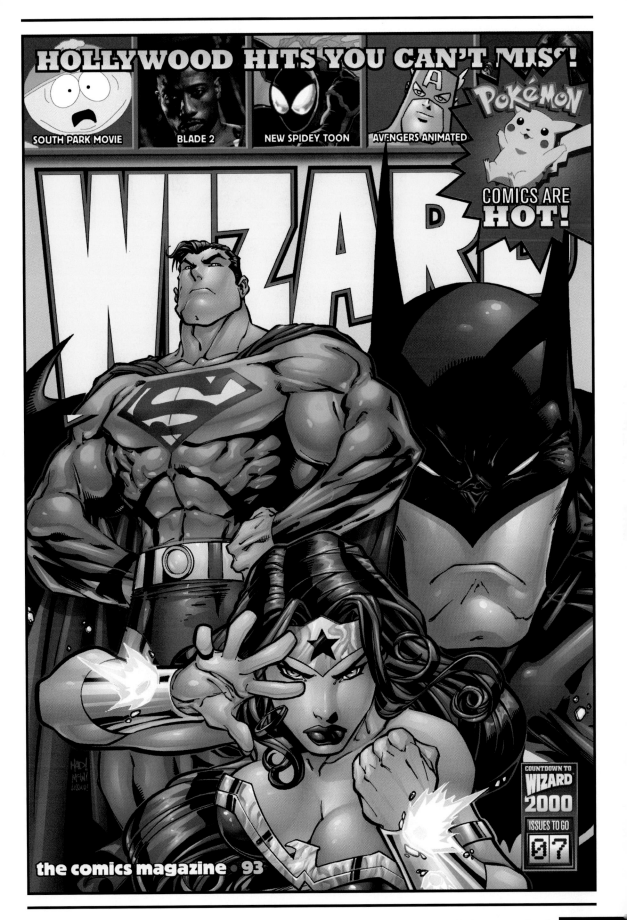

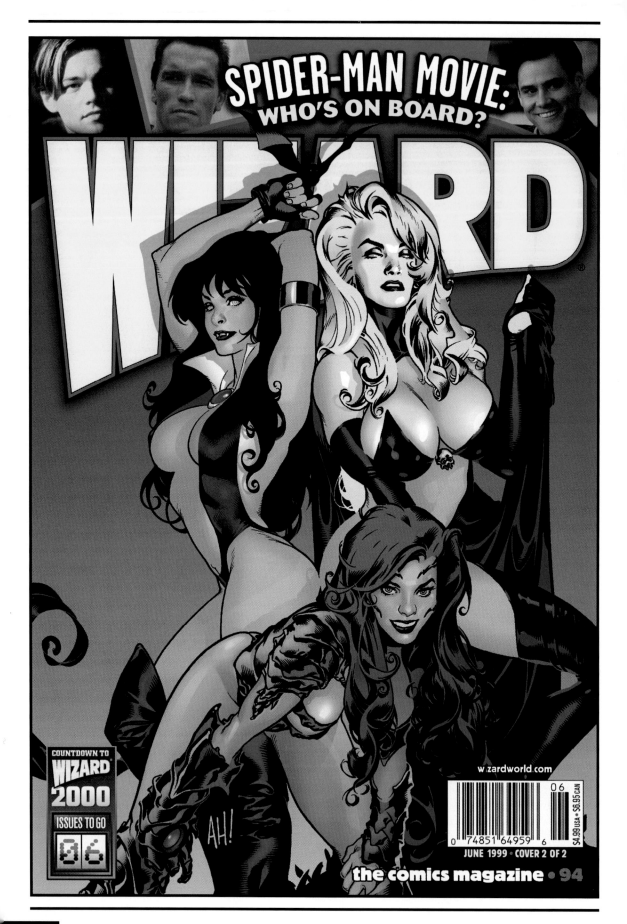

SPIDER-MAN MOVIE: WHO'S ON BOARD?

WIZARD

COUNTDOWN TO WIZARD 2000
ISSUES TO GO
06

AH!

w.zardworld.com

0 74851 64959 6
06
$4.99 USA • $6.95 CAN

JUNE 1999 • COVER 2 OF 2
the comics magazine • 94

94a

BAD GIRLS
(June 1999)
PENCILER/INKER/
COLORIST: Adam Hughes

Revisiting the hot babe motif from *Wizard* #83, artist Adam Hughes showcased three of comics sexiest superstars: Vampirella, Lady Death and Witchblade. The initial sketch **[directly below]** featured a more close up view that we almost went with, and the comical second sketch **[bottom]** made us laugh out loud.

94b

AUSTIN POWERS (June 1999)
PHOTO: Courtesy of Blake Little and New Line Cinema
Tying into "Austin Powers 2: The Spy who Shagged Me," this photo cover didn't quite meet sales expectations and—after one more experiment (*Wizard* #97)—we would better understand how to execute effective photo covers for the magazine.

95a

SOUTH PARK
(July 1999)
ART: Courtesy of
Paramount Pictures

After the success of the first South Park
cover (#80), we worked with Comedy
Central to run another to tie into the
"South Park: Bigger, Longer and Uncut"
movie release. Unfortunately, we couldn't
get any approved art that fit our cover
specifications. This final cover image
would be recreated by the Wizard Art
Department using the computer
program Adobe Illustrator.

95b

X-MEN (July 1999)
PAINTER: Alex Ross
We approached Alex Ross for another cover, but we
were hoping he'd paint a group of characters he had no deep love for: the
X-Men (especially Wolverine). He eventually came aboard, but with the
agreement that he'd do the "classic" new X-Men as the team appeared
back in *Uncanny X-Men* #107 (clockwise from top left: Storm, Phoenix,
Banshee, Nightcrawler, Cyclops, Wolverine and Colossus).

96a

WOLVERINE
(August 1999)
PENCILER: Brandon Peterson
INKER: Batt
COLORIST: Liquid Graphics

Wolverine vs. Pikachu? Uh, sort of. Here, Wolvie tears through the variant cover of #96 in an attempt to unleash vengeance upon Squirtle (off panel).

The initial sketch **[bottom left]** lacked action. The second sketch **[bottom middle]** was cool, but his arms covered too much of our logo, so we combined it with the third sketch **[bottom right]** to create the final version of the cover.

96b

POKÉMON
(August 1999)
ART: Courtesy of 4Kids

While Pikachu and Ash helped give us the best-selling *Wizard* issue of 1999, we chose to not run more *Pokémon* covers—despite protests from our marketing staff—as they skewed too young for our audience.

POSEY WOLVERINE

CUTTING THROUGH WALL WOLVERINE

JUNGLE FLORA WOLVERINE

97a STING
(September 1999)
PHOTO: Paul Schiraldi

Another non-comic related photo cover, this time of former WCW wrestler Sting.

True story: during the *Wizard* photoshoot for this cover (which took place backstage at a TV taping), wrestler Diamond Dallas Page ("DDP") hung out with the crew. He picked up the February '99 issue of *ToyFare* (*Wizard*'s sister publication focused on action figure collectibles), and opened to a page featuring a DDP action figure with the word balloon: "I'm the ugliest wrestler alive, but I'm still married to a Nitro Girl, loser!" DDP paused for a moment, then—as we each braced ourselves for his trademarked Diamond Cutter on the concrete—he laughed it off with a "That's true. And she's been in *Playboy*." Which she was. And we're still alone. So very, very alone…

97b SPIDER-GIRL/ BATGIRL
(September 1999)
PENCILER: J. Scott Campbell
INKER: Alex Garner
COLORIST: Liquid Graphics

We approached J. Scott Campbell with an idea that played to his strength: hot babes. You can follow the progression of sketches **[below]** as they move from dynamic to cheesecake poses.

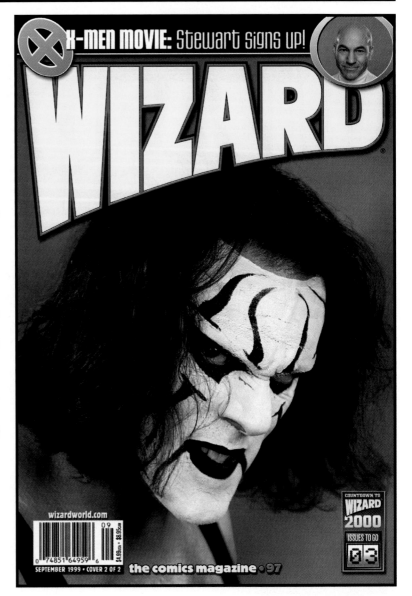

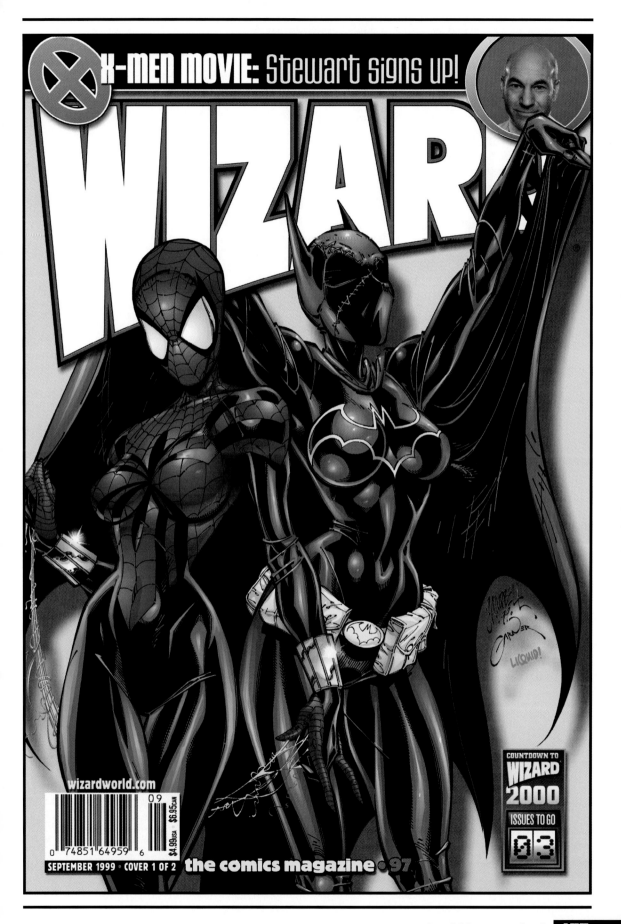

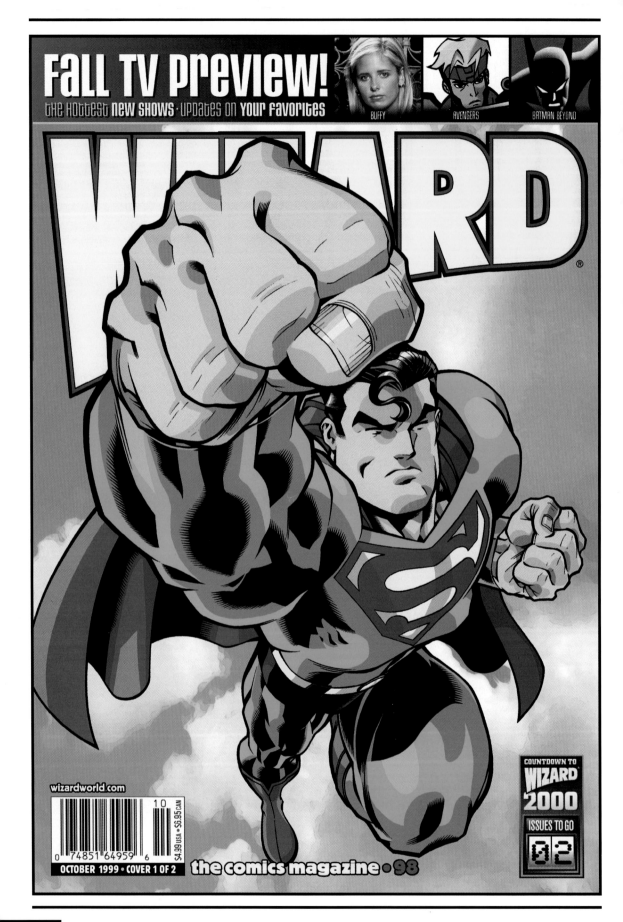

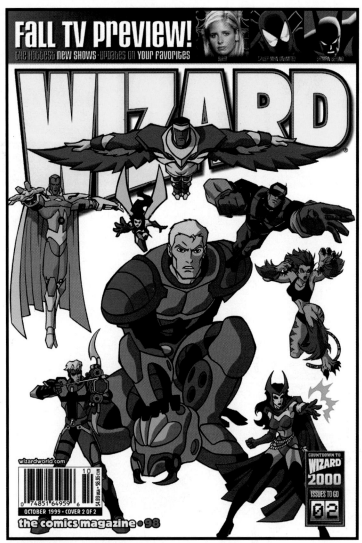

98a
SUPERMAN (October 1999)
PENCILER: Ed McGuinness
INKER: Jason Martin
COLORIST: Digital Chameleon

We asked McGuinness—then a Superman rookie—to draw a Man of Steel cover that had a classic feel to it. The initial sketches **[at left]** featured a "more powerful than a locomotive" riff and the timeless "Superpecs mightier than chains!" shot, but in the end we felt that a flying pose truly captured the essence of Supes.

98b
AVENGERS (October 1999)
ART: Courtesy of Saban Entertainment

Not quite as risky as our first Avengers animated cover (#85), this legit image of Earth's Mightiest Heroes was greenlit from the animation studio under one condition: the entire team roster had to appear on the cover. While well drawn, this cluttered cover is an example of why we usually shy away from layouts with more than two or three characters and instead prefer a more dominant cover image.

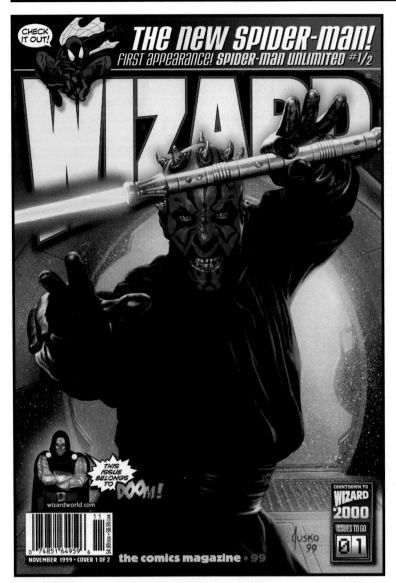

99a **DARTH MAUL** (November 1999)
PAINTER: Joe Jusko
While we originally pursued Lucasfilm for a photo of Star Wars baddie Darth Maul, all the available images were too dark or obscured too much of the character for our cover purposes. Plan B: we turned to painter extraordinaire Joe Jusko, whose ability to capture character likenesses and produce dynamic covers is second to none.

The initial sketch **[top right]** didn't have Maul looking ferocious enough, so with only a minor tweak to the lightsaber placement, we went with a pose similar to sketch #2 **[lower right]**.

This would mark Jusko's first *Wizard* cover (his first cover—a Deathlok image originally slated for issue #5, shown on p.11—never ran).

99b **BATMAN** (November 1999)
PAINTER: Alex Ross
What mega-Batman-event did this cover tie in to? None. Alex Ross just called out of the blue and asked if he could do a Batman cover.

Clockwise from bottom: Joker, Mr. Freeze, Penguin, Harley Quinn, Poison Ivy, Scarecrow, Riddler and Two-Face.

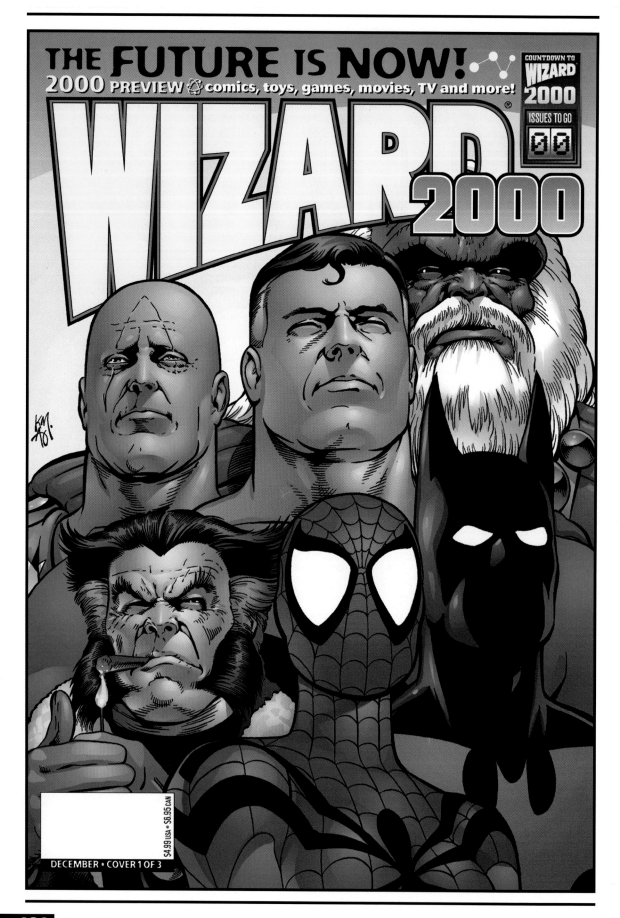

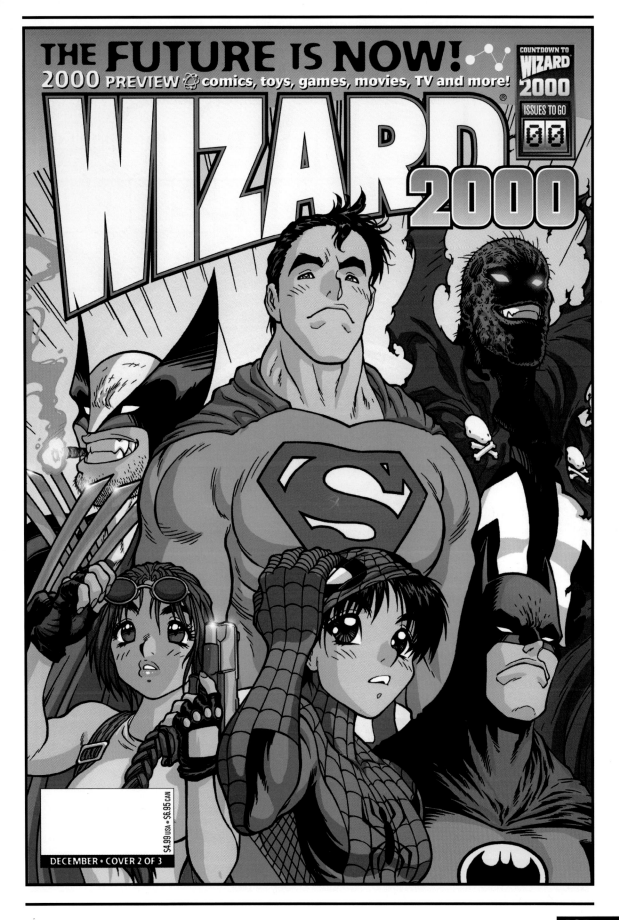

2000a FUTURE HEROES (December 1999)
PENCILER: Kevin Maguire
INKER: Al Gordon

COLORIST: Liquid Graphics

The theme for what were originally the only covers to *Wizard* #2000 (versions A and B) was "Future Heroes" composed by Joe Quesada **[top right]** and handed off to Kevin Maguire to pencil. (See p. 182 for cover image). Cover A featured the futuristic incarnations of comic's most iconic characters (clockwise from top left): *Earth X*'s Captain America, *Kingdom Come*'s Superman, *Future Imperfect*'s Hulk (Maestro), the animated Dark Knight of "Batman Beyond," the MC2 line's Spider-Girl and the "Days of Futures Past" Wolverine.

2000b SUPER MANGA (December 1999)
PENCILER/INKER: Adam Warren
COLORIST: Liquid Graphics

Running with the "Future Heroes" theme, this cover featured the hottest characters at the time rendered in the Japanese manga art style, a style that continues to heavily influence the world of animation and all of pop culture. (See p. 183 for cover image.)

Cover B features (clockwise from top left): Wolverine, Superman, Spawn, Batman, Spider-Man and Lara Croft (Tomb Raider).

2000c KINGDOM COME VS. EARTH X (December 1999)
PAINTER: Alex Ross

This piece was originally created as the opening art to a "comic projects you'll never see" feature inside the issue, but the Sales Department saw it and freaked. The art was resized **[above]** and a third variant was born.

The one-on-ones include X-51 and Reed Richards vs. Norman McKay; Daredevil vs. Deadman; Namor vs. Shazam; Captain America vs. Superman; Spider's Man vs. Jade; Hulk vs. Green Lantern; Captain Marvel vs. Starman; Iron Goliath vs. the Metal Man combined form; Medusa vs. Power Woman; Wyatt Wingfoot (Falcon) vs. Hawkman; Vision vs. Spectre; Thor vs. Wonder Woman; Skull vs. Lex Luthor; Iron Maiden vs. Trix; Black Bolt vs. Batman; Tony Stark vs. Aquaman and Venom vs. Nightfire

100a

THOR (January 2000)

PENCILER: Contest winner Carlo Barberi
INKER: Jimmy Palmiotti
COLORIST: Liquid Graphics

As part of a contest in *Wizard* #92, we called for art submissions from the fans where the winner would get a coveted art gig: drawing the cover to *Wizard*. After sifting through thousands of entries, we narrowed it down to two contestants: Ethan Peacock of Alberta, Canada, and Carlo Barberi of Monterrey, Mexico. Locked in a stalemate, we had them both draw a Thor image as our tie-breaker. Barberi's Thor sketches **[one shown bottom right]** would prove to be more dynamic than Peacock's **[bottom left]**. The final cover was identical to one of Barberi's other sketches.

As part of the prize package, we flew Carlo to New York, had him visit the *Wizard* offices and set up appointments for him to see Marvel and DC. As a result of the visit, he was hired as the ongoing *Impulse* series penciler within months.

The contest would prove to be an overwhelming success with several thousand submissions and has since become an annual tradition.

100b

SPIDER-MAN (January 2000)

PAINTER: Alex Ross

Our second homage to the cover of *Wizard* #1 (see *Wizard* #50 on p. 90). At first artist Alex Ross was hesitant to mirror Todd McFarlane's famous Spider-Man image, but when he was told it was for our 100th issue anniversary event, he came aboard and actually succeeded in making that pointy hat and robe combo look kinda cool.

And no, there are no plans to run a variant of this image on *Wizard* #150. Yet. ∎

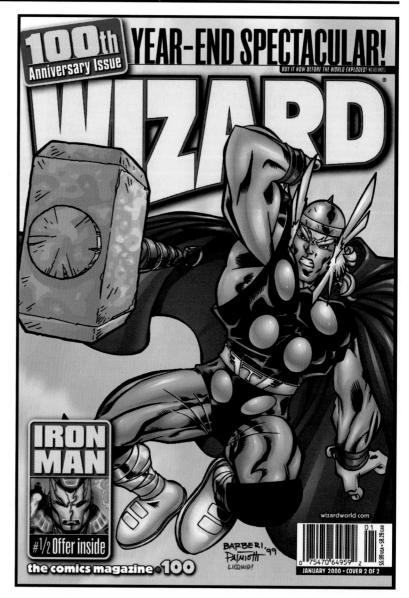

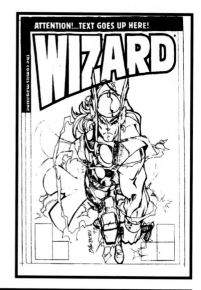

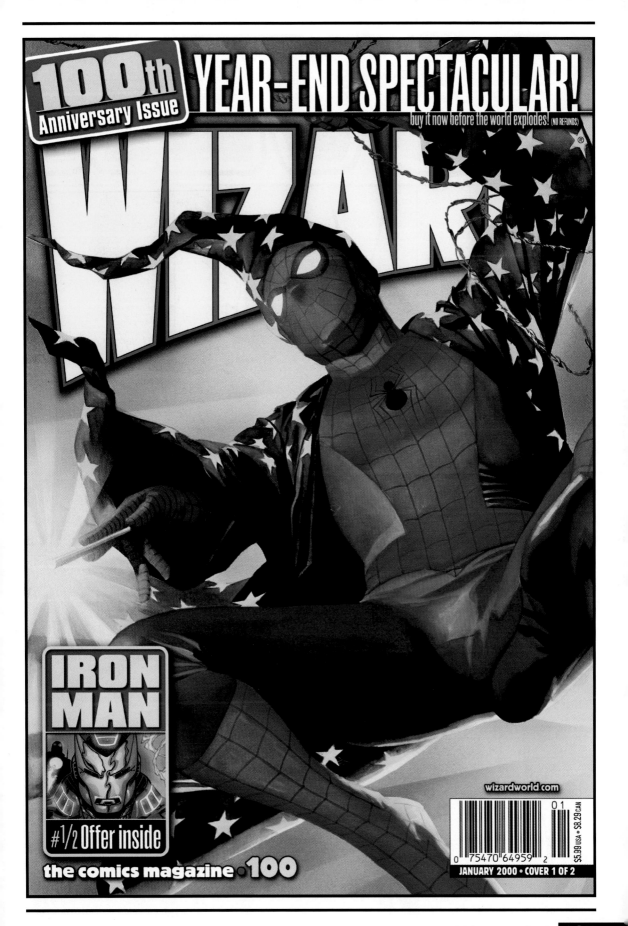

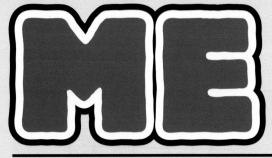

ME

We plot the five-month course of a 'WIZARD' cover from pipe-dream to publication

THINK DIFFERENT.

That's the mantra *Wizard* has learned through its cover creations since 1991. In fact, it's a luxury *Wizard* possesses, as evidenced by this Wolverine/Superman crossover cover [left] that combines properties owned by different companies. We push hard to get the best covers possible, and many an artist can attest that we never settle for anything less than perfection, even after the eighth round of sketches nor do we ignore what some might consider trivial details.

"The *Wizard* guys are the most specific people I've ever worked for," says occasional *Wizard* cover artist Kevin Maguire. "They have a VERY clear vision of what they want."

In fact, *Wizard* absolutely MUST think differently in order to thrive and survive. It's a harsh publishing world out there, and our covers compete with thousands of magazines ranging from *Time* to *Cigar Aficionado*, and each issue we produce needs to sport a cover that separates it from the pack. Our hard-and-fast guidelines: high contrast between characters and the background, bright colors, dynamic poses and catchy cover lines.

Because of the enormous importance of our cover images, they are determined by committee. Admittedly, a group dynamic can slow a process down, but it also increases our chances of finding that perfect image.

Clarity is critical. The cover must be clear in its presentation. If characters number more than two or three, the sense of clarity goes down significantly. That's why we usually keep it to one or two characters. Once we determine the cover character(s), we spin ideas to make it interesing—a cool fight scene, an interesting setting, engaging lighting and/or a dramatic camera angle. Many times we actually sketch out an idea for the artist to execute.

Every cover has at least three to five months of work from concept to final art to printed magazine. Here's a timeline to show how *Wizard* #85's Wolverine/Superman cover shook down…

FEBRUARY 27, 1998

For this cover, we go back and forth on various themes, and finally concoct an idea to team up a Marvel and DC character: Wolverine and Superman. The beauty of

being *Wizard* is that we can provide covers that other comic publishers can't due to sensitive copyright and ownership issues. Thanks to *Wizard* being a neutral party (think "Sweden," only with fewer clogs), we can work with all companies involved and—with the gracious go-ahead by the fine folks at Marvel and DC—fan-favorite "pipe-dream" images like this can become a reality.

We throw out some artist names, but the one that sticks is then-*Wolverine* penciler Leinil Yu, who had impressed us with a previous *Wizard* cover (*Wizard* #80, p.140).

Leinil says he'd love to do it—Superman being a favorite of his—and the furry mutant was already his turf. Since he's familiar with our cover layout (logo placement, etc.), he has everything he needs to proceed. We give Leinil a month to devise some sketches.

MARCH 31, 1998

His first round of sketches [images 1-4] gives us an idea. Leinil illustrated Wolverine with a cigar in his mouth, and we think, "Why not have Superman—a traditionally wholesome character—blow out the cigar?"

Leinil goes back to the drawing board.

APRIL 14, 1998

With Round 2 **[images 5-7]**, something isn't clicking (and it has nothing to do with image #5's "Supernipple"). The body language, the spacing between the characters…we aren't certain exactly what. We tell Leinil of our concerns, and he says he'd take another try at it, maybe go full-body with the poses.

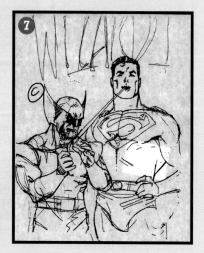

APRIL 15, 1998

Nope, this sketch **[image 8]** doesn't work either. At this point, it dawns on us that Leinil's syle would best suit a more splashy, action-oriented cover. This concept requires subtlety, particularly in the facial expressions. Regrettably, in order to execute the cover, we have to turn to another artist. We thank Leinil for his hard work and paid him for his efforts.

"I was disappointed," Leinil says today. Nice guy that he is, he understands what we were striving to accomplish.

The conversation now turns to a specialist who can nail subtle emotion with body language. We approach the one man who—with books like DC's *Justice League*—elevated the comic book facial expression to an artform: Kevin Maguire.

Revisiting all of Leinil's sketches, we couldn't help but notice that Leinil managed to space out the characters perfectly in his very first sketch **[image 1, p.189]**. We take Leinil's sketch and try to incorporate the cigar-blowing visual.

We fax it over to Kevin, who's worked from other artist's sketches before, and he agrees to take a spin at it, but not before asking:

"Why is Superman goosing Wolverine?"

Bwah-ha-ha-ha!

APRIL 22, 1998

Kevin reinterprets Leinil's concept and hits it outta the park [image 9]. The synergy works perfectly and—after insuring that the characters are respectfully handled and up to both Marvel and DC's quality—we have only one tweak. We ask Kevin to move Wolvie's hands up, so the blown-out match would be more visible [image 10].

"I've always looked at the characters as actors," says Maguire. "The better an actor is, the more wrapped up you get in what's happening to them. Facial expressions and body language is the way to portray what the characters are going through internally, which is as important as what's happening externally. It's another layer of storytelling."

APRIL 28

We receive the cover pencils and promptly ship 'em out to inker Al Gordon, a frequent collaborator of Kevin's.

MAY 3

Al's inked version arrives [image 11]. We make a high-resolution digital scan of the cover art and send it to coloring house Liquid Graphics via the Internet. The trick will be to allow the colors to enhance the subtle humor of this piece, rather than overwhelm it. The Liquid duo of Chris Lichtner and Aron Lusen know exactly what we're talking about.

MAY 5

Colors look good—only a couple minor tweaks to bring out more bright yellow in Wolverine's costume.

Many underestimate the challenge of clear cover coloring. When you have two characters of varied costume coloring, it's tough to come up with a background color that doesn't drown one or both of them out. Here, the challenge is to NOT use light blue—a popular background color because it often doesn't overwhelm the foreground—behind them. Because both characters have blue in their suits, they wouldn't pop off of a light blue backdrop.

In an inspired choice, Liquid uses a very light blue-green that offered much more contrast to help separate them effectively from the background.

MAY 6

After looking at the colored art one last time, we rack our brains trying to figure out why the image doesn't entirely capture the playful feel we're looking for. The Wizard design staff tweaks the near-final art **[image 12]** by adding a visible gust of "super-breath" blowing from Supes' mouth to the match **[image 13]**. Thank god we had Kevin raise Wolvie's hands, otherwise this effect would have streaked smack through the center of Logan's face rather than above his eyes. Almost there—the small touch of altering Wolverine's lit match to a smoky unlit match and darkening his cigar **[image 14]** seals the deal.

JUNE 15

The Editorial staff generates cover text blurbs, which are printed on the clear plastic polybag the magazine is sold in. [*EDITOR'S NOTE: Ever since Wizard #101, we have incorporated all cover text blurbs on the actual cover, not the polybag. Before #101, the polybag text had to "fit" at least two distinctly different covers each issue, making it an extremely difficult task to not obscure vital cover art. With multiple polybags being cost-prohibitive, printing text on the actual cover was a natural evolution of our cover process.*] Our Circulation Department looks it over, makes minor suggestions, and it's approved and shipped to our Design staff to add the finishing touches. The polybag—which needs extra time to print—is shipped out the door.

JUNE 21

The cover gets designed with the *Wizard* logo, bar code and polybag **[opposite at right]**. After a quick round of approval by a handful of internal department heads, we finish it a day ahead of schedule—a rare event.

JUNE 22

We ship the issue, including the cover, to the printer.

JULY 17

We finally receive "first-bound" copies of *Wizard* from the printer, which are the first 50 to 60 bagless copies printed. The colors appear slightly off-kilter in first-bounds because the ink on the printing press hadn't had sufficient time to set.

JULY 29

The issue hits comic stores. While fans get their first glimpse at the cover, the next five months worth of *Wizard* covers are already rolling through various stages of pre-production.

To this day, this piece—which took five months, two pencilers and a team of inkers, colorists and designers to bring to life—is considered one of *Wizard*'s fan-favorite covers. To us, it will always be—thanks to that Kevin Maguire fella—the "Superman gooses Wolvie cover." ■

Wizard would like to thank DC Comics, Marvel Comics and all the comic book publishers and artists who make this one very cool industry. We tip our pointy, starred caps to all of you.

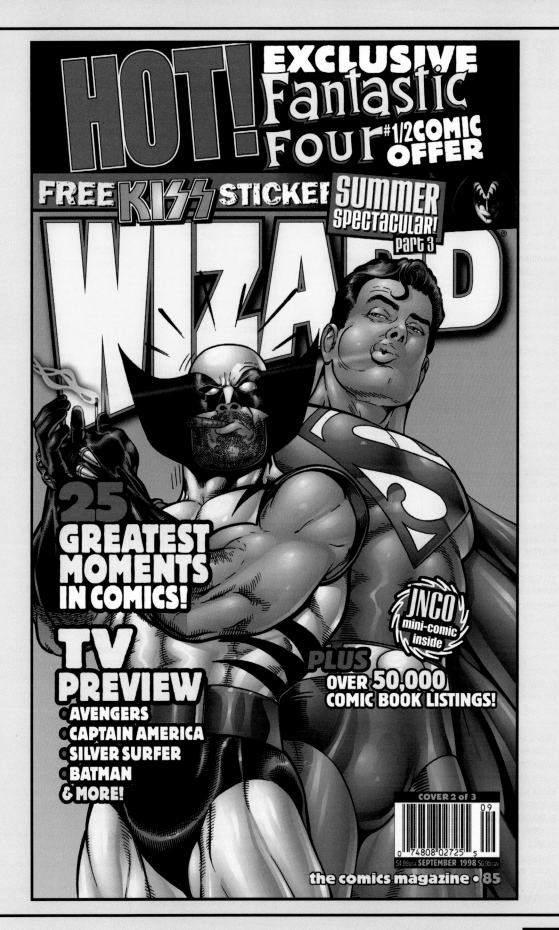

INDEX

All artists listed are either painters or pencilers. A single work that's spread over two pages is listed by the first page on which it appears. All characters are listed individually. Teams are only listed if two or more members from that team are present. No wagering.

WIZARD'S BIG COVERS BOOK, volume one, June 2003.
Please direct all editorial-related inquiries to Wizard Editorial Dept., 151 Wells Avenue, Congers, NY 10920-2064 (or Fax: 845-268-0053). Please address all subscription/renewal/comic and toy offer concerns to: Customer Service, c/o Wizard Entertainment, 151 Wells Avenue, Congers, NY 10920. One-year subscription rate is $29.95 (Canada $48.00, all other countries $70.00). All payments in U.S. funds only.
Any statements made, expressed or implied in WIZARD'S BIG COVERS BOOK are solely those of columnists or persons being interviewed and do not represent the editorial position of the publisher, who does not accept responsibility for such statements. All characters and artwork shown in WIZARD'S BIG COVERS BOOK are trademark and © of their respective owners.
WIZARD'S BIG COVERS BOOK (ISSN 1065-6499) is a special publication of Gareb Shamus Enterprises Inc., D.B.A. Wizard Entertainment, 151 Wells Ave., Congers, NY 10920-2064. Periodical postage paid at Congers, NY and additional mailing offices. RIDE ALONG ENCLOSED. Postmaster: Send address changes to WIZARD ENTERTAINMENT, PO Box 658, Yorktown Heights, NY 10598.
Entire contents © 2003 Gareb Shamus Enterprises Inc. The Wizard logo is protected through trademark registration in the United States of America. Publication information may not be reproduced in part or whole in any form without prior written permission of WIZARD ENTERTAINMENT and Gareb S. Shamus. PRINTED IN THE U.S.A.

Spiderman: TM & ©1991 Marvel Entertainment Group, Inc.
All Rights Reserved

WIZARD
ASHCAN EDITION

Months before the debut of *Wizard* #1 in September of 1991, we began laying the groundwork for the magazine with a black-and-white price guide distributed to retailers at comic book conventions across the New York Tri-State area (a more hands-on distribution process than the Internet...which wasn't really available to anyone at the time).

Originally envisioned as an all price guide magazine with little in the way of editorial content, this small pre-issue (shown here actual size with the original *Wizard* logo) was meant to build some equity into the then-unknown *Wizard* name.

And yeah...we photocopied and stapled together the copies ourselves.